The Modern In-House Lawyer:

Optimising Relationships for Growth and Success in an ESG Environment

Ciarán Fenton

Globe Law
and Business

Author
Ciarán Fenton

Managing director
Sian O'Neill

The Modern In-house Lawyer: Optimising Relationships for Growth and Success in an ESG Environment
is published by

Globe Law and Business Ltd
3 Mylor Close
Horsell
Woking
Surrey GU21 4DD
United Kingdom
Tel: +44 20 3745 4770
www.globelawandbusiness.com

Printed and bound by Severn, Gloucester, UK

The Modern In-house Lawyer: Optimising Relationships for Growth and Success in an ESG Environment

ISBN 9781787429529
EPUB ISBN 9781787429536
Adobe PDF ISBN 9781787429543

Table of contents

For Marian, Conor and Anna

Love, always

Special thanks to Dr David Donaldson, the doctors, nurses and staff of Belfast City Hospital Cancer Unit under whose wonderful care I achieved remission and started writing this book.

Endorsements

"Ciarán's insights are an excellent challenge for in-house lawyers trying to understand their role and manage their careers. His focus on in-house law as a growing area with changing priorities is timely and essential as in-house teams continue separation and evolution from their private practice roots."

Stephen Cooke, currently freelance general counsel operating through Konexo GC services and other channels; formerly MD in HSBC's legal function, HSBC global legal function COO and head of legal team supporting technology and operations.

"Few people understand the role of the in-house lawyer as well as Ciarán. This book is brimming with ideas and will encourage in-house legal lawyers to reflect on their role. Every in-house lawyer should keep a copy on their desk."

Thomas Crane, chief legal officer, International Personal Finance Plc; former general counsel and chief sustainability officer, Coventry Building Society.

"This book is conversational in style, easy to get into, hard to put down and full of gentle challenge and reflection for all of those who are, or who interact with, in-house lawyers. It is incredibly practical and does not shirk the difficult issues, including ethics and client pressure. It is well worth a thoughtful read."

Russell Deards, director of legal and compliance, Highbourne Group Limited; former head of legal/general counsel and company secretary in a number of companies since 2008.

"Reading this book is like being in conversation with Ciarán. Anyone who has spent time with him will recognise his authenticity. I like his direct style, the practical advice on relationship building, doing only seven things for seven dollars (not doing more for less), running the legal department as a business, speaking truth to power and holding that special role that comes with the practice of law in-house. As someone who aims

to create an environment where others thrive, I particularly like Ciarán's focus on finding joy and being happy at work 75% of the time, as per the title of his next book, *Most Mondays*."
Maaike De Bie, group general counsel and company secretary, Vodafone Group.

"Every decade or so, something comes along that changes the narrative of settled thinking. This book is as generous as a Wainwright walking guide, as well observed as a Bryson travel guide and as punchy and insightful as any McCormack 'What They Don't Teach You at ...' book. Fenton rests his views on a foundation of observing a generation of lawyers, and it is all here. If you are a lawyer, want to be a lawyer, are married to a lawyer, employ a lawyer, this book is not just important – it is essential."
Paul Gilbert, director, LBC Wise Counsel; former legal director and company secretary, United Assurance Group; former head of legal services, Cheltenham & Gloucester plc.

"I wish I had this book on my desk 20 years ago. It contains advice that is practical and useable in your day-to-day and should be required reading for all who are in-house lawyers or who interact with them."
Richard Given, general counsel, OpenPayd.

"In this book, Ciarán offers a no-nonsense guide to those who want to be the best in-house lawyer they can be. In pursuit of the ultimate prize of peace and joy at work, he sets his readers on an obstacle course to face the truth about themselves, the potential they have and the business in which they practise. This is not for the faint-hearted. Claiming to have read the book will provoke the question: so what have you done about it? Based on his personal and professional experiences, Ciarán systematically tackles the defences of the status quo. In their place, he provides the practical tools to build foundations for a future of fulfilment. Just as importantly, he signals why the status quo will be overwhelmed by stronger societal demands on businesses and those who counsel them."
Loughlin Hickey, co-founding trustee, A Blueprint for Better Business; former global head of tax, KPMG.

"Ciarán brings a refreshing and welcome sensitivity to the often macho world of corporate relationships, demonstrating that inclusiveness and kindness are actually beneficial to the bottom line rather than indications of weakness. I have long been an admirer of his perceptive and incisive guidance and this book crystallises his expertise."
Carolyn Kirby OBE, president Mental Health Review Tribunal for Wales; president Law Society England and Wales 2003

"This book is something to be savoured – dip into it slowly and deliberately as Fenton offers a number of thought-provoking insights on navigating the c-suite and the boardroom, as well as on how to improve in-house lawyer relationships. Moreover, he presents a refreshingly original take on both in-house counsel leadership and the management of in-house legal careers – making this an important read for those who want to grow and lead, with authenticity and purpose."
Mitchell Kowalski, author of *The Great Legal Reformation: Notes from the Field*

"This is a profoundly thoughtful and insightful book clearly drawing on years of intimate exposure to the profession. From my perspective at London Business School, I appreciated the many references to academic works. It is also intensely humane and kind. Ciarán says that he could never have written this book before his illness. I can see why. What comes across is a deep caring for the profession,

organisations and those who practise law in-house. Other professionals could also benefit from reading this book. His point about being aware of one's own and one's employer client's purpose and nurturing mutual understanding is pure wisdom. The book exposes severe weaknesses in legal training which prepares lawyers for careers as pressured 'micro-enterprises'. It has changed my perspectives. I wish I'd come across it decades ago."
Jeff Skinner, teaching fellow, strategy & entrepreneurship, London Business School

"This is an essential and timely book. Essential in its provision of practical techniques to master the art and science of delivering legal services within a business environment in which your client is also your employer. Timely in its presentation of in-house lawyering as indivisible from leadership at a time when businesses and professionals are called to greater standards of responsibility in and for society. It would not be an overstatement to consider that if a majority of general counsel, in any jurisdiction, read and applied a selection of the techniques in this book, the landscape of the legal sector and their lives would be positively transformed. That is not to say this is a book only for in-house lawyers and the many who work with them, including the decision makers who can maximise their contribution. It is for anyone interested in the mastery of themselves and their relationships at work and the doors this can open and, as needed, close."
Jenifer Swallow, lawyer and adviser to legal and technology businesses; former GC at fintech unicorn Wise and CEO of government-backed organisation LawtechUK

Acknowledgements

Writing this book was much harder work than I thought it would be before I embarked on this project. However, that task was made easier by so many people, not least those who are its subject: in-house lawyers. I have worked with hundreds over the years and many of them – too many to list here – helped me write this book through their courage in undertaking my programme. They allowed me to take them outside their comfort zones. They shared with me their personal histories – all a privilege to hear. They shared their strengths and weaknesses, hopes and even dreams. Some have become close friends. This book would not exist but for the fact that a large number of lawyers, in-house and out, took a chance on me. I'm grateful to them.

The first of these was Nick Deeming, who became a great friend. A hugely experienced GC, Nick asked me to research the business education of in-house lawyers and this led me to Paul Gilbert – who also became a great friend – and opened so many doors to me in the sector.

I want to thank Paul because he asked me to join the faculty of his widely respected LBCambridge2 programme for senior in-house lawyers. Paul is an alchemist who has brought together a diverse faculty and group of mentors to support around 16 in-house lawyers each year through a programme split between two residential sessions, with online mentoring between the sessions. The speakers and contributors include Justin Featherstone MC, Mandy Hickson, Fiona Laird, Martha Leyton, Claire Lomas MBE, Richard Martin, Professor Richard Moorhead, Kay Scorah, Jonny Searle MBE, Martin Shovel, Jon Sutherland and myself. The mentors include Katherine Bellau, Ray Berg, Dana Grey, Carolyn Kirby OBE, Chris Parker and Jonathan Smith. These extraordinarily talented people are now like family to me. I am grateful to them. The programme created an environment in which I could thrive in the sector and catapulted me towards new mandates with in-house legal teams and general counsel (GCs) – and in particular, my first two mandates with Richard Given and Jeff Medeiros, who afforded me wide latitude to innovate with them and their teams. I'm also grateful to Jenifer Swallow – a GC and a courageous leader within the in-house profession with whom I worked – for her ongoing support of me and my work.

I feel honoured and grateful that Richard Moorhead, professor of law and professional ethics, agreed to write the foreword to this book. Richard is part of the LBCambrideg2 faculty, where I came to know him over the years. His talks are extraordinary for their clarity, insight and rigour. His books and research – and, in particular, his work on the Post Office Horizon Inquiry, a major UK corporate scandal – set him apart in his academic field.

I have written this book against a background of changing views on the development of capitalism in society and a growing emphasis on the environment, society and governance (ESG), and on developing sustainable organisations. For deepening my understanding of these issues, I'm very grateful to Charles Wookey and Loughlin Hickey, co-founding trustees of independent charity A Blueprint for Better Business, whose purpose is to create a better society through better business. They exposed me to the developing canon of writing, to a widespread group of thinkers and to debates on these key issues.

My thanks also to my publisher, Sian O'Neill. Sian also took a chance on me by commissioning this book. She did so when I was in hospital for chemotherapy and a stem-cell transplant for mantle cell lymphoma in the summer of 2023. I was in isolation for long periods with no visitors. Her commission helped me through. Her support and guidance – along with those of my editor, Lauren Simpson – were invaluable. Thanks also to Carolyn Boyle for copy editing the manuscript.

To my two children, Conor and Anna, who encouraged and supported me throughout, a massive thank-you. Finally, and most importantly, I want to thank my wife Marian. A writer of far greater skill than I, she always supported me, believed in me and created an environment in which I could do my work. To her and to them: my love, always.

Foreword

Richard Moorhead
Professor of Law and Professional Ethics, University of Exeter

In one important sense, this book and Ciarán and I have come from the same place. That place is a room in Cambridge where, once a year, we hear and see sometimes extraordinary things. That place is, believe it or not, a leadership workshop. To an academic lawyer, that feels like an unlikely place for epiphanies or insights. But each year, over three-day sessions, in-house lawyers come and share their hopes; their dreams; occasional, very politely and modestly expressed pride; and sometimes the hints of failures for which they blame themselves. Each time I learn something about the profound importance, strength and vulnerability of being a leader in law in the corporate world.

In this book, you will see what Ciarán has learned from these people and from the consultancy and leadership work he has done with corporate boards and in-house legal teams. The epiphanies and insights that emerge during Ciarán's work with them can be dramatic. Delegates at the workshops experience being 'Ciarán-ed'. Grown men and women cry – not because they have been abused, but because they have opened up. There is, you see, a hypnotic directness to Ciarán's engagement with in-house lawyers in these moments. They are confrontations – albeit of the most considerate kind – with those he coaches, consults for and, now in this book, writes for. There is philosophy – not of the legal kind, but of a more fundamental hue. What is your purpose? Who are you really? Deep down, what do you really think you need to do?

As an academic lawyer, I might baulk at such emotive talk; but I do not, because Ciarán brings clarity, directness, thought and real experience to the conversation. He also brings, in abundance here, helpful ways of thinking about and behaving as a lawyer in business – perhaps the most intriguing and counterintuitive of which is that he thinks the legal function itself must be run as a business within the business, if you like. The legal function should have the equivalent of a chief executive officer, a chief technology officer, a chief operating officer and – God help us all – a chief financial officer (CFO).

A CFO? I am tempted here to make a joke that sometimes, ladies and gentlemen, Ciarán Fenton can go too far. I jest; but also, I do not. This book is ambitious in what it asks of lawyers. It covers wide ground. The in-house role in all its richness: psychology, ethics, business and relationships; relationships being the central thing, I think. His ideas will push you, help you and sometimes irritate and annoy you. For with clarity of thought comes the opportunity for disagreement and real engagement. This book is a manifesto for how to arrive at your own personal and business purpose: the plans you should lay; the behaviours you should develop. If you want to. If you need to.

The suggestions do not come from some dry academic even though much of what he says chimes with work from business scholars and behavioural ethicists. Ciarán has lived and breathed commercial life. Nor do the suggestions come from a lawyer. He knows – indeed expects – you to quibble, qualify, avoid, reframe and sublimate the real challenges he poses. Lawyers love, he knows, to avoid the general with the particular; to squirm away from the human with the analytical. They want to belong but be special. Yet he has heard dozens, even hundreds, of lawyers talk about the human dimensions when lawyering goes wrong. Here Ciarán's profound concern is with lawyers' ethics. Ciarán has heard from too many lawyers whose lives have been ruined, or close to, by the challenges of legal work gone wrong, where the desire to please, to find a way of not saying no, of going less slow, of doing more for less, has unpicked a life or lives.

Not all lawyers, even most, have experienced such terror; but many have experienced the ratcheting of pressure, the discomfort of being asked to do something which may be illegal or misleading, or which lacks integrity. Lawyers and legal academics are inclined to resolve these problems with rules, applying facts to words, dryly trying to determine that they did the right thing by parsing them just so. Ciarán's consultees have told him that really, it isn't like that at all. Legal leadership is more than words and rules; relationships, philosophies and behaviours are what count. Professional failures and successes are human failures and successes, not intellectual ones: they have human causes. And if you read this book, you'll see how Ciarán has put his finger very firmly on the human pulse that courses through our professional lives.

Introduction and context

1. The purpose of this book

This book is aimed at you if you are practising law as the employee of an employer client at any stage of your career in any jurisdiction, because the grammar of managing relationships at work is universal. I hope the book will help you feel more fulfilled. In addition, I dare to think the unthinkable: that this book will bring you more peace – even joy – at work. 'Peace' and 'joy' are words not always associated with the world of work generally, and with in-house lawyers specifically. I also hope that you will want to recommend the book to your employer client and to your external advisers. Your employer client should find the book helpful in creating an environment in which you can thrive – the responsibility of all employers – and to better understand the relationship between your role as an in-house lawyer and the creation of sustainable organisations at a time of increased emphasis on the environment, society and governance. Your external advisers – particularly your law firm advisers – will, I hope, use the book to help them give you a much better client experience and one in which they will feel incentivised to play a bigger role in the solution to your challenges at work than they do now. Finally, law students and those contemplating a career in-house or switching to an in-house career should find this book helpful in their career decision making and legal practice. That's the book's purpose. That's my purpose.

I use the words 'legal practice' deliberately. It's not a term I hear used frequently among in-house lawyers. Nevertheless, I'm asking you to consider – for reasons I set out in the book – that you will feel more fulfilled in your relationships at work if you accept that your primary purpose as an in-house lawyer is to practise law within the organisation in which you are employed. That employee lawyer/employer client relationship is complex. In this book, I attempt to unpack that complexity and help you manage its impact on your relationships and how you might better manage these to bring you peace and joy in your work most Mondays.[1] 'Most Mondays' is a concept I use in my work to describe feeling good most of the time, since it's impossible to feel good all the time. The words 'peace' and 'joy' may jar with you. You may even find them laughable or inappropriate. Don't. While these are not words that you and I usually see in the same sentence as the words 'in-house lawyer' – or indeed any lawyer – nevertheless, my purpose in writing this book is to help you set your bar high; to bring peace and joy to your work, now. 'Peace', because the world of in-house lawyers is not at peace with itself, with its regulators or with society. That absence of peace is creating harm to individual lawyers and to society, as evidenced by words of your colleagues and the research of academics set out in this book. 'Joy', because I witness more emphasis among in-house lawyers on the pleasure of achievement defined by others rather than on the joy of work which comes from within and leads to deeper fulfilment. Joy comes from within; pleasure from outside of you. I use the word 'now' because I want you to have peace and joy now – not next year, or when or if your profession reforms; but now, in this moment, in your practice of law in-house. I agree that is ambitious. But I am ambitious on your behalf.

Therefore, this is a practitioner's book for you as an in-house lawyer, focused on helping you manage your relationships better at work. It's what I do in my consulting practice for senior leaders at work in any role in any sector. I am not a lawyer, but because I have found significant demand for my help in managing relationships among in-house lawyers, I address this book to their needs. I believe people like you need to know seven things to feel fulfilled – to find peace and joy – at work most of the time. You need to know yourself – what you need, not just what you want; you need to know how to sell yourself and your ideas; you need to know how organisations work and how to work with others in them. You need to know how to lead and to follow; how to find and secure a role and when and how to leave it. Finally, you need to know how not to work, and how to take care of you and yours. This book addresses these needs.

2. How I stumbled into the in-house world

It's been my purpose in my consultancy practice to help senior leaders – including chief executive officers (CEOs), finance, marketing, sales, operations, technology and human resources directors (HRDs); chairs, non-executive directors (NEDs) and in-house lawyers – to be what they can be. I have spent more time with in-house lawyers than any of the other leaders because of a combination of accident and need. Need because they, of all the leaders I have advised, have – in my experience – the greatest need in managing their relationships. And accident because I stumbled into their world many years ago when I helped a general counsel (GC), who has since become a close friend, to find a new role and to look ahead to his post-corporate career. He asked me to research legal education, an area of interest for him. He felt that in-house lawyers were underprepared for business life. He wasn't wrong. That piece of research led me to conversations, work engagements and workshops with hundreds of lawyers, in-house and out, across the world – including an introduction to Paul Gilbert, a former GC and director of LBC Wise Counsel,[2] a consultancy supporting in-house lawyers. Paul – the doyen, in my view, of in-house consulting in the United Kingdom – invited me to become a member of the faculty of his LBCambridge2 programme for senior in-house lawyers.[3] I am still a member of that extraordinary faculty and have worked with scores of in-house lawyers from all sectors both through that programme and through my own contacts. At my first LBC2 programme, I met an assistant GC from a global financial services organisation. He gave me my first mandate to work with a global legal team. He also became a close friend.

My approach to that programme was to start with his leadership needs and then work with his direct reports and their teams across the world. I had by then developed a relationship management model which I had used successfully with CEOs, function leaders and main and executive boards. Using this model worked for him and for his team. The model involves a cycle of one-to-one conversations with each team or board member, followed by plenary sessions – often in off-site contexts. This model works well because of the confidentiality agreement I have in each one-to-one meeting and my approach to the plenary sessions. The agreement is that I undertake not to disclose any information from that one-to-one meeting to other team members without prior approval, save that I reserve the right to share my opinion about anyone or any issue to anyone. This transparent approach created trust and kept me out of trouble; and by the time the plenary sessions took place, I knew all the key relationship issues in the legal team and was able to facilitate – in a positive atmosphere – small changes in behaviour which, in aggregate, had a big impact on personal and organisational outcomes.

3. My early experiences working with in-house lawyers

In this first mandate with a global legal team, I had a breakthrough with the assistant GC regarding his leadership behaviour and how he could improve it, which he cites to this day and which he allows me to cite. He tended to prioritise pleasing others. We explored what, in his formative years, might have led to that behaviour – a process now common in emotional intelligence (EQ) thinking, a prerequisite competency in modern leadership; how he could make a new decision about that behaviour; and how to go about making small changes in his relationships now. He did. He says that the intervention made a significant difference to his career. Then I worked with the lawyer leaders of his practices and geographical teams across the world, as well as team members from other disciplines – particularly legal operations. I had my first exposure to cultural differences within legal teams. On one occasion, my somewhat direct approach to calling out behaviour startled one lawyer from a country whose working culture was not so direct. I quickly modified my behaviour.

When I completed that mandate, he introduced me to a colleague of his – a senior GC of a global division in that organisation who mandated me to help him reframe the relationship between the global legal function, which he led, and his employer client. This was a challenging but rewarding brief because it was with this mandate that I designed and pioneered the in-house legal function framework set out in this book, and which I have used ever since. I adopted the same approach with him and his team as I did in my first mandate – one-to-ones followed by plenary sessions – while also advising him to set up a legal operations board which included access to finance, technology and internal marketing/communications expertise. I also held extensive one-to-one interviews with board members and with risk functions in the employer client organisation. These interviews gave me an insight into the key problem I have witnessed everywhere I have worked and which I address in this book: a lack of clarity on the purpose of the legal function among in-house lawyers, their advisers, their employer clients and regulators.

My work with that in-house legal function culminated in a three-day off-site bringing teams together from across the world. At this off-site, I trialled an ice-breaking process on the first day which I have used since, which is to ask each attendee to share something non-controversial about themselves, but of which others on the team are unlikely to be aware. For example, one lawyer said they were obsessed with shoes and owned scores of pairs; another declared they were highly skilled in kickboxing; and a third had a successful track record in amateur drama. This session was followed by a relaxed dinner. By the time we met for the plenary session the next morning, ice was notably absent. At the plenary session, I learned that global legal teams struggle with the tension between central and local leadership; communication online – even before COVID-19; differences in regulatory contexts; and scarce resources, of course. But most of all, I learned that people are the same everywhere. They have similar feelings, needs and options for attending to these. I learned that lawyers are as confused by the word 'strategy' as those who are not lawyers and I resolved to address this issue in my programmes. Finally, I learned that what people want most from off-site experiences is to feel that the off-site was not a waste of time. They want follow-up actions listed on the final day and attended to without fail afterwards. The GC and his team had been initially sceptical about my approach, but to this day he is a key referee and champion of my work.

When that mandate was complete, I was asked by the global GC of the organisation to pitch to facilitate their annual global legal leadership conference involving the GC and senior lawyers from every division – over 100 lawyers in all. I won the pitch, despite the global GC's concern that I might be a bit too 'touchy-feely'. It took several weeks to prepare for the conference, during which time I was exposed to a range of issues of such international complexity it left my head spinning. But on one issue I was crystal clear: these lawyers – and lawyers generally – did not understand leadership from the perspective of managing relationships. I deigned to say so on the morning of the second day of the conference:

> Yesterday, I had a failure of courage. I should have said something, and I didn't say it. Maybe I was worried I was not going to get another mandate. But I will say it today: this is a global legal leadership conference, but I feel everyone is interested in legal issues and none in the leadership issues.

There was a long silence, eventually broken by one GC who expressed their displeasure at my comment. They felt offended, they said. I thought, "That's it! I'm finished!" But then I heard myself blurt out: "Hands up those who agree with me." I felt sick as no hands went up, initially. Then one or two went up; then suddenly, to my great relief, most hands went up. My intervention didn't change the course of the conference, but it sowed the seeds of the nature of my work with in-house lawyers over the many years that followed. I wanted to make a difference to this profession of invariably bright and brilliant "insecure overachievers", as described by one academic.[4] I was fascinated by them.

4. My formative years

Maybe I wanted to be one of them. I almost chose law at university but studied business instead. I majored in law in my business degree and particularly enjoyed contract law. In my corporate career, I spent much of my time working on deals with lawyers. At Pearson Plc, the publisher, where I was commercial director of Financial Times Television, I had great fun flying around the world with my boss negotiating draft business television news memoranda of understanding and returning to London to face the withering eye of our GC. "You can forget Point 6, Ciarán, that's not happening!" she would say. "The rest is fine." I learned so much from her. We also negotiated a multi-party news deal and I spent a lot of time in meeting rooms with senior private practice lawyers fencing line by line with each other. A few exchanges remain like earworms in my head. One would advance with, "... not without prior written approval ...", to be met with, "... such approval not to be unreasonably withheld or delayed". The first would concede. I often wondered why they tried it on. Or the difference between "best endeavours" and "reasonable endeavours". 'Best', apparently, includes to your own detriment. One lawyer I know says this argument is spurious. They rarely agree. But I enjoyed watching their sparring. But it was not until ITN – one of the United Kingdom's leading news providers, where I was managing director of its archive and IP exploitation division and spent two years leading the negotiation for the management and exploitation contract of the entire Reuters Television Archive – that I learned how a good relationship between principals can cut through some of the legal sparring. I developed a very good relationship with the other side on what was a very sensitive IP asset deal and I managed to get the deal over the line, as the lawyers say. It was my biggest deal as an executive in business and an education on so many levels, and it increased my fascination with lawyers. I also learned about the fine hierarches within the legal profession. But I learned that if I were to help lawyers and barristers – and I worked with several of the latter – I had to understand what motivated them. Hierarchy and relative brightness matter to them; although I must say that I find the notion of terms such as 'baby silk' and 'senior junior' in the Bar truly hilarious.

Perhaps my fascination was also that I knew I could help them with an issue in which I was skilled and they weren't. I could feel useful. Their training had, it seemed to me, rendered them helpless, at times, in their relationships at work – not that you will hear them openly acknowledge this helplessness. Perhaps it was because I had been poor at managing my relationships at an early age because of experiences in my formative years, and had learned to change and wanted to pass that on. I'm not sure. Indeed, I'm often asked about how I came to do this type of work – a blend of relationship, career and change management. People ask if I have a psychology degree – I don't – because they see me working closely with feelings, needs and the impact of formative years' experiences on current behaviour. Not long ago, these issues were taboo topics at work. But today, senior leaders are expected to develop high EQ. The business press – Naomi Shragai in the *Financial Times*, for example – routinely covers the relationship between leadership behaviour in business and formative years' experiences. Psychotherapy and mindfulness are now accepted routes to fulfilment.

I was in therapy for several years dealing with the impact of my formative years. This mainly focused on my experiences at primary school, where I was fast tracked two years ahead – aged seven in a class of nine-year-olds – resulting in unsurprising psychological damage; and then at a boarding school monastery for nascent religious teaching brothers, where I was sent aged 12 and which made my internal life even worse. It also centred on my experiences of 1960s Ireland, which was a very different place from what it is today. I was fortunate in my therapists – mainly highly skilled *Gestalt* and psychodrama specialists. They helped me recover myself 'in the Now' – a concept best explained, in my view, by best-selling author Eckhardt Tolle in his book *The Power of Now*;[5] but also, as a collateral benefit, I came to understand the difference between relationship and change management consulting – which is what I do – and therapy, which I don't do. The difference is that I do not use the tools of therapy – working with transference, projection, attachment issues and so on. I don't use silence as a therapeutic tool. I use it to learn more. If someone cries in my sessions, as they frequently do, I ask them why they are crying. A therapist would wait. But I will ask them whether they are aware of the impact of their formative years' experiences on their current relationships at work.

5. How I started in leadership consulting

I'm also asked how I got into this line of work. The trigger was in the early 1990s, when I met Mark McCormack at the World Economic Forum (WEF) in Davos. I was fortunate to attend the WEF several times, despite my youth, because I was commercial director at Financial Times Television, which had a relationship with the WEF. Mark McCormack had written many famous books, especially *What They Don't Teach You at Harvard Business School*[6] and *The Terrible Truth About Lawyers*.[7] I was fascinated by the work he was doing taking care of senior sportspeople – not so much in his role as agent, but in helping them. I figured that leaders at work receive insufficient support and I resolved to start a business to support them as if they were micro-businesses. My opportunity didn't come until 2002 when, following redundancy, I set up a consultancy, initially focused on career management. I failed to scale it because people wanted me, and I wanted them to want everyone in the consultancy. So, I reverted to a solo model and moved into change management – particularly for boards and executive boards, which is the focus of my work today; although I still do a lot of one-to-one work. I enjoyed the work and more of it came my way.

Following those initial three mandates at that financial services organisation described above, they referred me to the GC of the global division of a telecommunications business. I repeated the process there over a few years and added new elements to my approach. For example, at an off-site with the senior leadership team of the legal function, I trialled my pre-coffee break mantra, repeated three times: "Is anyone in this room left with an itch they have not scratched; a view not expressed; a feeling not articulated?" I would ask this once, twice ... and, invariably, before I reached the third time, one member of the team would reveal a key unresolved issue. On one occasion, one person said that they felt aggrieved that another member of the group accepted deadlines from "the business" – a term which intrigued me, and still does – without first checking whether the legal team had the capacity to meet those deadlines. After the coffee break, I facilitated a discussion on the issue using an approach – Feel/Need/Do (see Chapter 1)

– which most lawyer clients have found particularly useful. One client, a private practice lawyer, said the tool had changed his life. He said that he had disconnected with his feelings during his private practice training and early years at work. The approach – developed by others and described in detail in this book – connects people with their feelings, needs and options. It works.

And so, through word of mouth, I gained a reputation for making a difference not just to in-house lawyers and their teams, but also to private practice lawyers and their boards of management. I worked with the leadership team of the London office of an international law firm, with the leadership team of a regional law firm and one-to-one with many managing partners. Meanwhile, my practice with other function leaders, boards and executive boards was growing. On one occasion, a GC helped me to secure a mandate with the executive board of their employer client at a point of inflection. Points of inflection were and are my entry point to work with boards and senior leadership teams. These include changes at the top – a new CEO, for example – or a rapid growth phase or post funding round, to mention just three.

Early in my consulting career, much of my work came from career management or so-called outplacement mandates paid by organisations or by individuals. I developed a model to manage job searches, interview processes and the first 100 days of a new role for all senior roles across all sectors, including some work in the public sector. Soon, lawyers – in-house and out – were contacting me to manage their careers crossroads. These included those voluntarily looking for new roles and those forced out by circumstances – some because of bullying by their employer clients. On the private practice side, one international law firm hired me to manage the departures of some of their equity partners – some voluntary, some not. I learned a great deal about private practice work, and that's how I picked up mandates working with managing partners who wanted me to help them and their senior leadership teams.

6. My shock at the 'resign or conform' culture in-house

The more work I did in the legal sector, the more I understood it and the issues that dogged it. These had been highlighted by academics for many years – particularly by Professors Richard Moorhead and Stephen Mayson (whose research I quote later) and by LBC Wise Counsel director Paul Gilbert. I was shocked. The headline was then clear to me that in-house lawyers were struggling to act with independence because the clients that they advise are also their employers. They have latterly confirmed their pain and the consequent harm being done to society publicly, as set out in Chapter 6 and in the appendices to this book. I started to speak and write about what I was witnessing. I was invited to speak at conferences and legal summits, and to write articles. I spoke at the Association of Corporate Counsel European Summit in Munich and, later, in Rome. I spoke at GC summits in London and in Dublin, including *The Economist* GC Summit. I was invited to speak at in-house workshops, and to speak at and chair The Law Society GC Summits. I wrote articles for The Law Society website. In 2015, I published a pamphlet, *The GC-CEO Relationship Post Global Financial Crash: Flourish or Flounder?,*[8] in which I proposed the reframing of that relationship. I set up a GC/CEO forum at that time, but it failed to take off because I wasn't in as good a position then to engage with boards. I also trialled a six-month helpline for distressed lawyers – titled #lawyersbacks – which I chaired. Their stories were shocking, not least because they felt alone and unsupported. I wrote several long pieces for *Modern Lawyer*, a quarterly journal published by Globe Law and Business, the publisher of this book. The most important of these – "Inherent tension in-house: defusing the law department timebomb during a pandemic" and "Lawyers, and their regulators, can make or break the ESG movement"[9] – are included in Appendices 1 and 2 because I hope they will help you to understand not only my take then on the evolution of the legal function, and my own and others' concerns about its future at that time, but also how my views have evolved since then – especially since I had cancer and my views on everything changed.

I also wrote blogs[10] and posted my views on LinkedIn and Twitter. Then

– in a chance exchange on Twitter with a number of parties with an interest in the topic, including the UK Solicitors Regulation Authority (SRA) – I asked whether the SRA had carried out a thematic risk review into the independence risks faced by in-house lawyers. The SRA replied on Twitter that it had not done so, and that if I wanted to propose this I should get in touch. So, in February 2020 I wrote to the SRA to propose that it "do a Thematic Risk Review on risks faced by In-House Counsel in accordance with your Enforcement Strategy and for the reasons set out in the Twitter exchanges, which also reference academic research and case law". Others supported this proposal on the Twitter thread. In due course, the SRA replied stating that:

> [we] continue to consider a thematic review on in house lawyers' independence. Unfortunately, we are unable to put a timeframe on when a decision will be made and when any such review will be undertaken. This will of course, need to be considered against other thematic reviews we are currently undertaking and considering.

It was clear to me that nothing would change until in-house lawyers came together and called for change, or perhaps set up their own institute for in-house lawyers ('the IIHL', as I have dubbed it) – an idea that has been mooted by some in-house lawyers over the years.

Then, in the United Kingdom, an inquiry into a horrendous corporate scandal – the Post Office Horizon IT Inquiry – was established in September 2020, which included questions about the behaviour of lawyers.[11] Professor Richard Moorhead gave evidence to the inquiry, wrote about the issues arising on his blog Lawyer Watch[12] and was informally supported by a group of lawyers and consultants – including me – facilitated by Paul Gilbert. One member of that support group, experienced GC Jenifer Swallow, then led a group of lawyers and consultants – including me – in a debate on best next steps for the in-house legal function. During that debate, she and I sought to engage with employer clients and to move the debate by publishing in June 2022 a Contract Amendment Template[13] for in-house lawyers (see Appendix 3) designed to help restate their independence obligations in their employment contracts. Then in March 2023, the SRA, having carried out a thematic risk review, published a report entitled *In-house Solicitors Thematic Risk Review*.[14] Thirty-three in-house lawyers, led by Jenifer Swallow, were so concerned by the SRA's failure to address in its report the pain experienced by individual in-house lawyers and the harm being done to society that they wrote a letter responding to the report and published it on LinkedIn.[15] That letter (set out in full in Appendix 4) was – to my mind, at least – historic. In-house lawyers had broken – as one in-house lawyer called it – their *omertà*-esque silence. Nothing would be the same again: previously, I and others could only write and speak about what we observed or what was contained in anonymous research; but now we can quote the lawyers and they bear out our observations.

Meanwhile, I also spoke at events not linked to in-house lawyers directly but on related matters – notably on creating sustainable organisations and environmental, social and governance (ESG) issues to the MSc students at the University of Bologna and on the same topic to similar students at Robinson College, Cambridge. I spoke at a World Commerce & Contracting Association[16] conference in Arizona on purpose beyond profit – a topic in which I have an ongoing interest. For example, since its foundation over 10 years ago, I have been associated with and worked with a charity focused on a purpose beyond profit in business: A Blueprint for Better Business.[17] I was forming a view of the world of business and law which some business and legal leaders were ready to hear, others not. What was clear to me was that where I could add most value was in helping people manage their relationships better at work.

7. How this book came about

"What is top of mind for you today?" This is the first question I ask my in-house lawyer clients in one-to-one sessions and at workshops. I find that their answer is not about legal matters, processes or regulations, but about their relationships. These cause them considerable pain; although usually, they don't use the word 'pain'. That's a feeling. Lawyers are trained to eschew feelings. I have written this book, therefore, for three reasons. First, having worked with hundreds of in-house lawyers, I feel that in-house lawyers need a relationship management reference book tailored to their specific needs within organisations and as regulated professionals. Often, I wished I had written down my experiences and processes with GCs and teams, but never found time to so. Then I had cancer; and while in hospital, I received an email from Sian O'Neill at Globe Law and Business – the publisher of this book – to say that they had a book of mine in their summer sale. I wrote back to say that they had made a mistake: they could not have a book of mine on sale, since I had not written a book; but I added that if they were interested in a book of mine, this is the book I would write. They asked me to pitch formally. I did, and the editorial board approved the publishing contract.

Having cancer changed my life and how I have approached writing this book. I think I would have written a different book before I had cancer. You will see for yourself the difference in tone between my articles in the appendices, written before I had cancer, and this book, which I wrote during and after my chemotherapy treatment and stem-cell transplant for mantle cell lymphoma, which took over a year in and out of hospital for many weeks at a time, in isolation and without visitors because of COVID-19. The experience stretched my mental resources to their limit. It also changed my values and my views on almost everything, including in-house lawyers and how I write. I look back on some of my earlier blogs with embarrassment. Cancer has made me less strident about the issues I care about. I still care deeply about these; but my approach now – and the first reason I wrote this book as it now is – is to try to help to fix, not to point; to influence not to hector; and to focus on fulfilment and systemic change as a function of finding peace and fulfilment – and yes, even joy – at work. Second, external advisers need to find new ways to deepen their relationships with their in-house clients if they wish to differentiate themselves. They can achieve this outcome best by helping their in-house clients navigate their relationships better. This is a two-way street. In-house lawyers would benefit from a more empathetic and emotionally sophisticated out-of-house relationship. Third, having worked with many senior executives, chairs and NEDs who are not from legal backgrounds, I feel they need to understand more fully the legal function and how to manage their relationship with it. Indeed, my experience is that lawyers and those who are not lawyers operate as if on different planets. This is not a good foundation for building sustainable businesses. Writing about the relationship between in-house lawyers and their employer organisations, Professor Stephen Mayson wrote in his *Independent Review of Legal Services Regulation* that "there is little doubt that a tension is inherent in this relationship when the client for legal services is also the adviser's employer".[18]

I have witnessed this tension at close quarters in my consulting practice. In many instances, the relationship is dysfunctional. Employers of in-house lawyers could benefit so much from understanding the legal function better – particularly in how it can help create more sustainable organisations. In-house lawyers would then benefit from being understood. I'm finding that organisations are increasingly asking in-house lawyers to lead on ESG issues; that they in turn need support with this additional workload and perhaps encouragement to believe they can make a significant leadership contribution to changing the relationship between business and society. I acknowledge that some are reluctant leaders in this regard, feel in a weak influencing position and query whether organisations are taking ESG seriously. I address these challenges in the book.

Law firms were traditionally the focus of attention and support from the profession and regulators, but the number of in-house lawyers and their responsibilities have increased exponentially since the 2008 Global Financial Crash. In addition, the role, purpose and behaviour of in-house lawyers have increasingly been in the spotlight due to corporate and political scandals leading to increased regulatory scrutiny. These factors have put in-house lawyers under heightened stress in managing their relationships with themselves, with their teams and with their client organisations, and vice versa. These trends are validated by academic research which I quote in this book. Lawyer stress is on the increase, according to international studies also quoted in the book; and I have witnessed this stress in my consulting practice. Much of the stress emanates from challenges in managing relationships.

The final title of the book was a joint effort with the publisher. They understand the legal publishing world. I understand relationships at work, particularly regarding in-house lawyers. Together we agreed on: *The Modern In-House Lawyer: Optimising Relationships for Growth and Success in an ESG Environment.* I apply the adjective 'modern' to 'in-house lawyer' to indicate an expectation of the highest standards of contemporary relationship management thinking, especially in relation to EQ, the components of which are empathy, self-awareness and the ability to negotiate needs productively. The term 'in-house lawyer' refers to regulated professionals practising law in-house, whether solicitors, barristers or attorneys. I use the word 'practice' deliberately and encourage readers to use the word more frequently to describe their role, because the use of that word will lead to more honest, deeper and richer professional relationships at work in-house.

I had mixed feelings about using the word 'optimising' in the strapline of the book. It's bordering on management-speak and I have tried – not always successfully – to avoid jargon in the book. I also feel that the word is transactional in tone and jars a little with the word 'relationship'. That said it's a word that the legal and business worlds use and understand; and indeed, I propose relationship contracts between team members in the book. I used the word 'reframing' as a step to 'optimising' and I hope this comes across as sensible. The word 'growth' primarily refers to the personal development and EQ growth of in-house lawyers, organisations and society in their interactions with business. Implicit is financial growth, which is essential, like breathing. While the word 'success' is in the strapline of most how-to books for the usual reason that financial and career success is a universally appealing concept, I primarily use it to mean fulfilment at work – a core theme of this book. My main motivation for writing the book is to help in-house lawyers feel happier in their careers. We agreed to use the acronym 'ESG' in the strapline because of the growing emphasis on environment, society and governance in business and the extent to which ESG is a here-to-stay issue – one on which employer clients are increasingly asking their in-house lawyers to lead. Its use is also an upfront call to you to always honour society in your practice of law in-house.

8. The structure of this book

In Chapter 1, I set out tools, principles and models on how best to manage your relationship with yourself which I have tried and tested with in-house lawyers over many years. They like these. In Chapter 2, I discuss how to manage the business of your career as an in-house lawyer. Chapter 3 is about managing your relationships at work. Chapter 4 is about how to understand and view the key relationships in any organisation. Chapter 5 is about how to lead a legal team, and how to understand and work with a client employer main and executive board. In Chapter 6, I address the tension in the relationship between you as an in-house lawyer and your client which you advise, but which is also your employer. Finally, in Chapter 7, I propose a framework to reset the relationship between in-house legal departments and their employer clients.

The book is conversational in style. I've written it imagining I am speaking mainly to in-house lawyers at all stages of their careers at a workshop or conference. I repeat myself several times, for emphasis and for those dipping into the book. If you are an experienced GC, some of the content will be well known; but I hope I can help all in-house lawyers in terms of managing their relationships, whether you are at the start or at the end of your career. Whether you read the book cover to cover or dip in, I hope this book makes a difference to you finding more fulfilment – peace and joy – in your lives. Cancer has taught me that this is all that matters.

Notes

1   Ciarán Fenton, *Most Mondays: How to Find Joy at Work Most of the Time, From Your First Job to Your Last*, the working title of my next book.
2   www.lbcwisecounsel.com/.
3   www.lbcwisecounsel.com/events-and-workshops/lbcambridge2/.
4   Laura Empson, *Insecure Overachievers*, BBC Radio 4, 26 September 2018, www.bbc.co.uk/programmes/b0bkqy1l.
5   Eckhart Tolle, *The Power of Now: A Guide to Spiritual Enlightenment*, Yellow Kite, 2001.
6   Mark H McCormack, *What They Don't Teach You at Harvard Business School: Notes from a Street-Smart Executive*, Bantam, 1984.
7   Mark H McCormack, *The Terrible Truth About Lawyers: How Lawyers Really Work and How to Deal With Them Successfully*, Beech Tree Books, 1987 (also published in another edition as *What They Didn't Teach Me at Yale Law School: The Terrible Truth About Lawyers*, Fontana Press, 1988).
8   Ciarán Fenton, *The GC-CEO Relationship post Global Financial Crash: Flourish or Flounder?*, Oaktree Press 2015.
9   Ciarán Fenton, "Inherent tension in-house: defusing the law department timebomb at a time of pandemic", *Modern Lawyer*, October 2020 and "Lawyers, and their regulators, can make or break the ESG movement", 9 *Modern Lawyer*, October 2021. See Appendices 1 and 2 for the full text of the articles.

10   www.ciaranfenton.wordpress.com.

11   www.postofficehorizoninquiry.org.uk/about-inquiry.

12   Professor Richard Moorhead's blog "Lawyer Watch", https://lawyerwatch.wordpress.com/.

13   Jenifer Swallow and Ciarán Fenton, "Strengthening governance through in-house lawyer independence. A note for in-house lawyers and their employers". First published on Jenifer Swallow's blog, June 2022, www.jeniferswallow.com/posts/in-house-lawyer-independence-employment-amendment-letter.

14   SRA, *In-house Solicitors Thematic Review*, 14 March 2023, www.sra.org.uk/sra/research-publications/in-house-solicitors-thematic-review/.

15   Letter signed by 33 general counsel led by Jenifer Swallow, "GC Response to SRA In-house Solicitors Thematic Review", published on LinkedIn by Jenifer Swallow, March 2023, www.linkedin.com/posts/jenifer-swallow-a1a4482_gc-response-to-sra-in-house-solicitors-thematic-activity-7044634751093071872-lF6_?utm_source=share&utm_medium=member_desktop. See Appendix 4 for the text of this letter. Also available at: https://docs.google.com/document/d/e/2PACX-1vTsOgvh0qvOWK_kFXUUnqBct5bxHQuV3jzhDU9QwSbUUY59rJx4vjD1Pc5e9RSbZOt94emhyTrWNERS/pub.

16   World Commerce & Contracting Association, www.worldcc.com/.

17   A Blueprint for Better Business, www.blueprintforbusiness.org/.

18   Stephen Mayson, *Independent Review of Legal Services Regulation*, The Centre for Ethics and Law, UCL, 2018, www.ucl.ac.uk/ethics-law/publications/2018/sep/independent-review-legal-services-regulation.

Chapter 1: You – how to manage your relationship with yourself

1. Introduction

This chapter covers the principles, tools and models that I use in my one-to-one sessions and in my workshops with senior leaders – including in-house lawyers – in all sectors about managing one's relationship with oneself. All your relationships at work start with *you*. You are the first party in every relationship. Get that relationship right and you have a strong chance of managing your relationships with others successfully. Get it wrong and you become a major part of your relationship problems. I find that the most popular tool in my programme among in-house lawyers in managing their relationship with themselves is 'Feel/Need/Do', so I start with that approach. I guess lawyers like this approach because their legal training eschewed feelings in favour of thinking. They know intuitively, despite their legal training that – as Eckhart Tolle writes in *The Power of Now*[1] – their identity is not bound up their thinking: "You are not your thoughts." However, due to the pressure of their work, they often conflate thinking with their identity. So, I find they like reconnecting with their feelings.

One lawyer said to me that the Feel/Need/Do approach changed his life. He said that over the last 20 years he didn't *do* feelings. He felt that he had, in his words, to suck up emotional pain. He regretted that he had waited so long to deal with his supressed feelings. He listed the benefits of the approach, which included lower stress levels; he took on less work; he noticed more often when he felt short tempered; he took more breaks – I suspect he delegated more; he said that he improved his business relationships by telling people about the Feel/Need/Do process and his experiences of applying that approach in his relationships at work.

2. Feel/Need/Do

This tool is based on the work of Marshall Rosenberg, among many other writers and psychotherapists who focus on feelings in the moment as a starting point in managing your relationship with yourself. I found the process changed my life when the *Gestalt*[2] therapists with whom I worked used it in their one-to-one sessions with me and in workshops – particularly psychodrama workshops – which I attended in the early 1990s. However, I recommend Rosenberg's book, *Nonviolent Communication: A Language of Life*,[3] because it is accessible in presentation, is a bestseller and I know lawyers who like it. Lawyers, particularly but not uniquely, are trained to avoid their feelings and need to reconnect with them to manage their relationships productively. Typically, they go straight to Do, skipping the Feel and Need steps. They might consider connecting with what they feel, what they need in relation to that feeling and what options are available to them to meet those needs. A typical example is the in-house lawyer who expresses fury at being criticised and not connecting with their deeper truth of hurt, disappointment and fear; and how, by connecting with those deeper feelings, they can surface for themselves deeper needs, better options and outcomes. Rosenberg was an exponent of the application of a version of Feel/Need/Do in resolving conflicts. He tells the story of the man who said he needed a divorce because he believed his wife was taking his hard work for granted. His wife, on the other hand, said she never saw him and that their relationship lacked intimacy. Rosenberg facilitated him and his wife to do a version of

Feel/Need/Do. The outcome was that the husband learned that he could connect with his feelings of being taken for granted, with his need for appreciation; and that while divorce was one option, there were other options, including negotiating behaviour change with his wife. His wife connected with her loneliness, her need for time and intimacy and her options for negotiating how these needs could be met. Neither needed, necessarily, a divorce. Rosenberg believed that if we express our needs, we have a better chance of having them met. Unresolved conflicts are invariably about unmet needs not expressed. You can meet your needs more productively in your relationships at work if you start by connecting with your feelings – all of them – and with your needs, and then list your options to have these met productively. Dashing off an angry email is an option but is unlikely to be productive.

Unresolved conflicts within boards, teams and joint ventures abound. They are deeply damaging. I know this from my work with clients. I have used Rosenberg's technique on many occasions by facilitating behaviour change contracts between board and team members. Chief executives and other leaders – including in-house lawyers who lead – could benefit from Marshall Rosenberg's views on freeing themselves from old programming. By this, he means our conditioning. The most powerful conditioning comes from our parents. Rosenberg proposes a literacy of needs as an antidote to conditioning by becoming conscious of our needs. Mindfulness experts – particularly Eckhart Tolle[4] – tend to agree that this is the first step in behavioural change. Many people behave unconsciously at work. Once they become aware, something shifts for them and others. Once they connect with their feelings, they can articulate their needs. Needs are feelings, not actions. If my client says, "When my direct report does not take responsibility for his team, I panic because I (desperately) need to succeed and I depend on him," those are feelings. Whereas a statement such as, "I, therefore, micro-manage him" is an action. To paraphrase Rosenberg's formula: "When A happens, I feel B, because I'm needing C and, therefore, I would like D."

Frequently, people under stress – like you practising as an in-house lawyer – may act viscerally and may not connect with their feelings or assess all their options based on their needs. For example, anger is a shallow feeling which frequently masks deeper feelings of fear, anxiety or hurt. The classic situation of a furious CEO letting rip is well known in corporate lore. What feelings lurk beneath their fury? Others use psychological tactics such as shame. I once worked in an organisation where the CEO simply had to use what we called his 'D-word' to exert complete control – as in: "Ciarán's results are very disappointing this quarter." Shaming was institutionalised, as it is in many organisations. His bosses, probably, had shamed him during his ascent through his corporate career. He knew no other way of working.

Many leaders believe, as the saying goes, that the behaviour that "got me here will get me there". Why wouldn't they? They know no other way of behaving. So many forget that the process of getting to the top is different from the processes required to succeed at the top. In-house lawyers who get to the top are often excellent lawyers but not necessarily excellent leaders.

So, the first step in Feel/Need/Do is to check in with what you are feeling. Angry? Frustrated? Humiliated? Anxious? Insulted? Undermined? Jealous? Bullied? Or several of these? Anger usually comes first. It's the shallowest of emotions, we're told. Take time to check out what emotions lie underneath those nearest the top. This is hard to do. The temptation to reply instantly – through the red mist – feels irresistible. Resist it. You will not regret it. I assure you that investment in this step will pay off. So, let's say you have received an email from your boss and you feel anger/frustration/fury at a top level; but by checking in with yourself, you find that your deeper truth is that the email has made you feel anxious/humiliated/undermined. The email hasn't made you feel anything, as psychotherapists will point out. Nothing, short of physical force, can make you do or feel anything. You feel what you feel. A good start, therefore, is to say to yourself, "I feel angry, frustrated, humiliated and anxious," and not, "That email made me feel ...". The intent of the sender may not be to wind you up and humiliate you. You don't know. It could be about them. They too may feel anxious and exposed, or not. In fact, all you know is what's written down, or not; and since few of us are Tolstoy when it comes to business communications, it's not a stretch to assume you haven't a clue what the writer intended. So, breathe deeply. This is an important step. Your emotions are felt in your body. Your body needs air. If you connect with your breathing, you will connect with your body, which – in mindfulness terms – connects you with the present moment: as Tolle calls it, "the Now". He says that there is no past, no future – only "the Now". So, all that matters is what you feel in the moment of reading that email from your boss – neither your thoughts about what happened with your boss in the past nor your analysis about what your boss might do or not do in the future, but only what is happening for you in the moment of reading the email: for example, "I feel angry and extremely frustrated; but also I feel anxious, a bit humiliated and alone." Or whatever. Don't ignore your deeper feelings, no matter how painful they feel to you. Face them and face them now.

Then, what do you need in this moment of reading the email in relation to the feelings you have faced? Well, speaking for myself, I'd like not to feel all those feelings – and soonest, since I tend to obsess about emails and texts for days. Most clients feel the same way, save for the psychopaths and the most Obama-esque. But if you take time to confront your needs having faced your feelings, the solution options will present themselves to you more easily: for example, "I need my boss to stop treating me like this"; and/or "I need my boss to understand that their take on the issues is not correct"; and/or "I need more time and/or resources to meet my boss's needs"; or whatever. What matters is that you are aware of your feelings fully in the moment of feeling them. There are no right or wrong feelings or needs. They are what they are. For sure, they may or may not be reasonable or realistic; but they are what they are. All our emotional pain comes from our failure to accept what's happening in the present moment. That's at the heart of the mindfulness approach to life and work. When you have accepted your feelings and needs in relation to the email from your boss, you can then set out the options you have in achieving those needs. For example, do nothing? Sulk? Spend all night drafting a stinker of a reply? Plot revenge? Cry? Or figure out what part of your pain is about you, what you need from your boss by way of

You may be surprised to find that by telling people what you feel and need, you get your needs met more often than not. That's what work is about: getting your reasonable needs – not always wants – met, productively, most of the time.

explanation/action; and then ask them, or not? But take responsibility for your own morale. Try the last one. It works.

Whatever you do, try not to respond in writing. Ideally, meet – and if you can't, then pick up the phone/arrange a Zoom – and ask lots of questions to check out what's going on. Invariably, it will be different from what's going on in your head and heart. Then, and only then, can you decide what to do, including telling the other person what you feel and need, or not. You may be surprised to find that by telling people what you feel and need, you get your needs met more often than not. That's what work is about: getting your reasonable needs – not always wants – met, productively, most of the time.

3. Seven principles

When I launched my consultancy practice over 20 years ago, the ratio of my one-to-one work versus board and senior leadership teamwork was much higher than it is now; and it was mainly in career consulting (or outplacement, as it is called), because that's where I could earn most money quickly. Organisations hired me to support what they called 'leavers' to help them find another role after being made redundant, or worse. Individuals hired me to do the same work, but they paid me from their own funds or from their redundancy packages. A third source of revenue was, and is, end-of-career senior leaders seeking to build a portfolio of non-executive directorships. A fourth segment were those in mid-career at some point of personal inflection or career crossroads – for example, bored at work and looking for a career change, looking to launch their own consultancies or crisis based (eg, one client needed to re-evaluate their purpose in life after the death of a family member).

I can't recall when exactly, but early in those first few years I listed seven principles about relationships at work in which I held strong feelings based on my experiences, on my reading and on my work with clients. I published these in my marketing materials:
* Your career is a unique micro-business – one in over 7 billion in its uniqueness. You're not a human capital asset.

- Your job is a joint venture with an organisation for increasingly brief periods.
- Organisations will hire you if you're the least risky choice, not necessarily the best.
- Your organisation's purpose, strategy and behaviour (PSB) are key to its success.
- Your personal PSB is key to achieving personal fulfilment.
- Your organisation consists of unique career micro-businesses with their unique personal purpose, and so it follows that your purpose and the purpose of your organisation are interdependent – even if it doesn't feel like that sometimes.
- Small changes in behaviour have a big impact on personal and organisation outcomes.

I have applied these principles in my practice for as long as I can remember. I explore them in depth throughout the book, and two here.

4. Your career is a unique micro-business

Your career is a unique micro-business – one in over 7 billion in its uniqueness – and the sooner you accept this reality, the better I believe your relationships at work will be. You are a unique professional services firm on legs, selling your services for cash and soft benefits. All of the art and science of business apply to you. The only differences between you and other businesses are size and complexity. What is up for debate is the extent to which uniqueness matters in a world where power and money appear to trump uniqueness. Based on my experience, you, as an in-house lawyer, are probably underutilising and underappreciating your uniqueness; and so is your employer client. You have more power in your relationship with your employer client than you think you have. You can rebalance your relative power by paying more attention to the business of being you. If you lead others, and you accept the principle of uniqueness, then you can create a better environment for the people you lead to thrive. Academics have long confirmed that every person has a unique brain anatomy. This uniqueness is the result of a combination of genetics and life experiences. But you know this already and you don't need research to confirm it. There are nearly 8 billion people on Earth and there are none the same as you. Not one. Why would you not at least consider exploiting that advantage? The reason is that organisations fear that they can't cope with uniqueness, so they do everything in their power – and therefore in their language (management-speak) – to cleave to generic rather than individual language, despite lip service paid to the once-popular fad of bringing your whole self to work. At one conference I attended, at which the then novel idea of bringing your whole self to work was discussed, one delegate quipped: "That's the last thing we want from our employees – what a bloody nightmare that would be!"

It should be easier for in-house lawyers to appreciate that they are unique micro-businesses. Many, after all, to quote one wry commentator, are "not entirely displeased with themselves". But I find that is true only on one level: when they are sure of their ground. Otherwise, imposter syndrome – on which more later – is common. Beneath the swagger and bravado of some or the quiet practice of others lie a deep insecurity and pressure to conform and an ever-present fear of being found out – by which they mean to have made a mistake, to be deemed not bright enough or to seem insecure. My advice to you, therefore, is simply to bring into your awareness as frequently as possible the reality of your career as a unique micro-business, even if initially at least you are sceptical about the practical application of that principle over time. By bringing into your awareness – another mindfulness term – I mean that you simply notice that you are unique. No lawyer can rebut that fact. Simply notice regularly that no one has had the same timeline as you – you've had a unique childhood, education and career to date. By recalling that fact regularly at work and over time, you will find that your attitude to your career shifts – subtly at first; then it will dawn on you that accepting it will change your life. It's that fundamental.

5. You are not a human capital asset

Your job as an in-house lawyer is a joint venture between you – a micro-business – and your employer client for a term. You are not a human capital asset. No one is. Check your body. Can you see barcodes? Check your employer client's asset register. Are you on it, with an annual straight-line depreciation? No. Is human capital a line on your employer client's balance sheet? No, to all the above. Of course not. Accountants would, if they could, have found a way to put you on their balance sheets by now. They haven't because they can't. Human capital doesn't exist. Never has. Never will. No amount of metaphorical mind-bending will change that fact. No organisation owns you. Of course, you are – technically speaking – a human resource to the extent that you are human, and you are a resource to your organisation. But people see themselves as neither human capital assets nor human resources, and that's what counts. Once – and I repeat this story several times in the book for those dipping in – when facilitating a workshop with a group of HRDs, I asked, "Hands up if you love being a human resource." No hands. So, avoid whenever you can in your practice of law in-house the term 'human capital', which has no place in an ESG-compliant organisation; support your HRD in becoming a chief of staff; and remind your CEO, if you get the opportunity, that they are responsible for treating people as individuals with dignity. You are not a human capital asset; nor, in ESG terms, are you a human resource. Your organisation exists only in law. Otherwise, it's a construct. Some CEOs say that people are their greatest asset. They're not assets. You, whose key tool is language, can lead the way in discouraging that term.

6. Parent/Adult/Child mode

This tool is based on the well-established theory of transactional analysis made popular by the bestseller *I'm OK, You're OK*,[5] which was based on academic research by Eric Berne in the late 1950s. The model is used widely in a range of contexts today. I have seen his three ego states in action in my work with individuals and boards: Parent, Adult and Child. Berne believed that our interactions are transactions. I apply this concept to individual and boardroom relationships by facilitating small change behaviour contracts between board members. For example: "I will micro-manage less if you take more accountability." Agreed? That's an example of an Adult-Adult transaction. Frequently I find that employees personify and parentalise their organisations – that is, speak of them of as if they are people with ultimate power. Once

I worked with an executive board and during the first session it became clear to me from the language they used that they didn't feel in control of the business. I fed back to them that when they referred to the business, they did so as if it were a powerful person or persons – often the main board – outside the room. They looked baffled. I asked whether they realised that they, largely, controlled what the business did and how it did it on a day-to-day basis. Again, bemusement. Their reaction is understandable. Society has created organisational power structures which are dominated by shareholders in private companies and bureaucracies in public organisations. It's no wonder that executive board members feel or behave as if they have no control. Even NEDs say to me that they have influence, but no power – even though company law gives them explicit power and an obligation to exercise that power. The risks to society – which includes employees, including in-house lawyers like you – of some or all members of main and executive boards behaving in Child mode with respect to the Parent organisation represented by the most ruthless CEO supported by their enforcer(s) can be catastrophic, as the inquiries into corporate scandals have revealed.

I find that in-house lawyers vary in their Parent/Adult/Child behaviour in practising law in-house. Some behave in a healthy Adult-Adult mode and others in Parent-Child mode. However, in managing their relationships in-house, particularly with their employer client, I find that some can revert to Child-Parent mode. They can parentalise their employer client, appearing to abandon their power as professionals with asymmetrical knowledge. They focus on pleasing their employer clients, doing more for less – an imprecise catchphrase that became popular on the in-house conference circuit – and performing what many of their number call the 'diving catch': a cricket term for diving for the ball full stretch with no regard for personal injury. I witness many in-house lawyers inflict injury on themselves and on colleagues in this Child-Parent behaviour. This pattern is not behaviour which can be changed overnight. My advice is to start by simply noticing your behaviour: as Tolle[6] calls it, "watching the thinker". As soon as you start behaving consciously, by noticing your behaviour, the act of noticing leads to change. I recommend Tolle's book to my in-house lawyer clients because I have found it powerful in addressing my learned behaviour. I also recommend, in this regard and generally, a book given to me by a GC – *Daring Greatly*[7] by Brené Brown – which argues that showing our vulnerability is a strength, whereby the courage to show up for ourselves can bring purpose and meaning to our lives. Her Ted Talks deservedly top the charts.

7. Formative years' decisions and your timeline

I developed this model because I needed a simple way to work with clients on the now well-established principle of the link between current behaviour in your relationships and your formative years' decision making. I ask a simple question of clients: "What were your formative years like?" I ask you now. You can use a simple scale which I use with clients to explore this issue. Imagine a line on a page with zero on the left and 10 on the right and two marks between zero and ten – one at four and another at seven. That leaves three rough formative years' experience scores:

0	4	7	10

- Score 7–10: I use the popular TV series – in my youth at least – *Little House on The Prairie* and *The Waltons* as metaphors to capture formative years' experiences characterised mainly by loving and nurturing contexts in which you could negotiate your needs and have them met, or not, reasonably.
- Score 4–7: A mixed experience. Sometimes like *The Waltons* and sometimes very definitely not. Some good experiences; some significant pain.
- Score 0–4: Very tough. The opposite of a *Waltons* experience.

Then I ask clients their timeline. I ask you to do so now.

DOB	18/21	Now	RIP

What was your birth year? That's the start of your timeline – date of birth (DOB). At what age did you start to act independently of parents/guardians? Say, 18/21 – that's the first milestone on your timeline. What behavioural decisions did you make in your formative years up to 18/21, if any? Examples: "I decided to keep my head down/to be the class joker/to trust no one/to be everyone's friend/to please/to win at everything"; or "I don't recall making any decisions." To what extent do you feel you have made new behavioural decisions in adulthood? You haven't changed much? You have changed? You don't know one way or another? To what extent do you feel your current behaviour will determine the rest of your life? It will? It won't? You haven't thought about it? You feel stuck?

If your DOB is the first mark on your timeline and age 18/21 is the second mark, then NOW is the third mark. Three years' time is the fourth mark and your death (RIP) is the final mark. The issue for you and all of us is: what new decision could you make now in how you manage your relationships at work different from those you made in your formative years, if any? Will you make it now? Not tomorrow or next week or next year, or when things are calmer at work, but now? Where do you want to be, and what kind of person do you want to be in, say, three years' time – a reasonable career interval – which period would set the foundation for the rest of your life? My purpose is not about analysing precisely what happened during a client's formative years and embarking on a process to deal with it – a complex task best performed by therapists – but to address at a high level only the extent to which they are still playing out decisions they took during their formative years. This high-level analysis has become common in the business press for some years. For example, Roger Jones, in the *Harvard Business Review* (2016), wrote:

> *Does your CEO remind you of your bullying older brother? Or the mother who always refolded your clothes because you didn't do a good enough job? Or the emotionally distant father who never praised you? Watch out: Chances are your CEO is recreating the very same dynamics that shaped his early family life. The entire executive team, and its mission, may suffer unless the CEO recognizes it and takes conscious steps to change his subconscious behavior. My work with top executives has shown that deep-seated, sometimes irrational fears*

Since your career is *a business –*
not like *a business – you can apply*
all the art and science of business
to the business of your career.

can skew their decisions and their ability to execute company strategy. But I've found another influence, equally deep-seated, that affects how they deal with others in the C-suite: their earliest interactions with family members and friends. Research has shown that our early family experiences often re-emerge in our adult life interactions with others, including those in the business world. Families, after all, are our first "enterprise," and our parents and siblings are our first "management team." Early family life affects how leaders respond to pressure and react when team members compete for their attention.[8]

Many years ago, I worked with a board whose CEO was a notorious micro-manager. He made the life of his team miserable. This emerged in a board game I use with boards, called "Least Likely to Say", which I describe later. His colleagues on his board said that he was least likely to say: "Don't mind me … Just crack on … All I need is the occasional call or email." On the contrary, he was most likely to look over shoulders, constantly seek updates and, above all, meddle. His micro-managing had a severely negative impact on his team and was ultimately a risk to the business in achieving its desired outcomes.

I have worked with many micro-managers, but this CEO had high emotional intelligence, in that he acknowledged that micro-managing was his main behavioural weakness at work and in that he was self-aware enough to say that in his formative years his parents would not tolerate failure of any kind in any context. I frequently say in my workshops that if we don't allow our children to fail, they will grow up to be micro-managing leaders. He had decided as a coping strategy not to trust anyone because he felt he couldn't rely on anyone to do anything that might impact him without his constant oversight. This behaviour persisted into adulthood.

However, it is possible to make a new decision – or a re-decision, as academics such as William Glasser[9] term it – regarding behaviour. In our work together, the CEO agreed to make a small change in his behaviour: to micro-manage 10% less (ie, 10 times less out of every 100 interactions). When I checked in with him after six weeks or so, he was so driven and competitive that he proudly reported: "I have delivered not just a 10% reduction in my micro-managing behaviour, but a 20% reduction!" It was true. He said that his colleagues were happier. I said, "No surprise there." He said he now had more time. I said, "No wonder, because micro-managing eats time." But crucially, he was learning that he could trust his colleagues more and recognised that the decision he took in his childhood, while appropriate at that time, had served its purpose then and he could take a new decision in the light of adult circumstances. You can do the same. The positive impact on your relationships at work will, I assure you, more than pay for the minimum 10% behaviour change investment you make.

8. Soft balance sheet

Since your career *is* a business – not *like* a business – you can apply all the art and science of business to the business of your career. My clients like to use the language of business – especially in-house lawyers who want to feel part of the business – to map career issues. In my model, you have a hard balance sheet and a hard profit and loss account, just as your employer client business does. The only differences are the amount of money involved and the relative complexity of your career business. By 'hard balance sheet' and 'hard profit and loss account', I mean those relating to cash. But you also share a problem they too confront, which is the challenge of managing soft assets and liabilities. By 'soft', I mean intangible.

The soft balance sheet is a tool I developed which has worked well with lawyers and with other leaders. It sets out their strengths as Assets A, B and C, and their weaknesses as Liabilities D, E and F. The value of the tool is the relationship between the D-Liability – your outstanding behavioural weakness – and your A-Asset, your hidden strength. My case study on the micro-managing CEO illustrates the tool. His micro-managing behaviour – his D-Liability – acted as a lid on his ability to trust others, which was his hidden A-Asset. The soft balance sheet which I use with clients to map their intangible assets looks like this:

Soft Balance Sheet

Assets
A Latent skill, competence or passion
B Key strength as viewed by others
C Domain knowledge

Liabilities
D Outstanding behavioural weakness at work as viewed by others
E Career contextual; weakness 1
F Career contextual; weakness 2

So, your A-Asset is that skill, competence or passion you currently do not show the world but resides within you and is currently hidden beneath your D-Liability. Your B-Asset is that which you know, and everyone knows, is your key strength at work. Your C-Asset is your domain knowledge – your areas of expertise.

Your D-Liability is your outstanding behavioural weakness at work, as agreed by third parties. Your E and F-Liabilities are career-contextual liabilities: anything – including unconscious bias – that might work against you in an interview, such as leaving school early, not going to university or spending a lifetime at one company. Your D-Liability is a lid on your A-Asset and is a function of your formative years' experiences. Connecting with your A-Asset is the key to career fulfilment. The purpose of my work is to help people connect with their A-Asset. In constructing your soft balance sheet, start by addressing your D-Liability: your outstanding behavioural weakness at work as might be expressed as a consensus by colleagues. The reason you should start with your D-Liability, and why I do so with all new clients, is because personal and organisational fulfilment comes from small changes in our worst behaviour as perceived by others. If you confront your D-Liability and make small changes to it, then you can work, lead or follow in a much more fulfilling, rewarding and – from the point of view of the organisation – productive manner. We all have one outstanding behavioural weakness at work, although my wife maintains that I have more than one. I've given up arguing with her that

that is grammatically impossible. "You can only have one outstanding anything," I say. She rolls her eyes.

Do you know what your outstanding behavioural weakness at work is? If not, why not? If yes, are you sure it accurately reflects the consensus of your colleagues? Or are you kidding yourself? Many people don't know what they don't know about themselves. My Dad, when he was alive, would have called this compound ignorance. Over the years, I have encountered every possible D-Liability based on self-assessments and the views of third parties. Before the Away Day – a full day which I spend with each new client – I telephone at least three referees whom they appoint and ask them five questions. I've asked these same five questions for as long as I can remember. They work for me, and you can use them too.

- "What is my client's best skill at work? What are they good at doing?"
- "Separately, what do they enjoy?" I find that many people – particularly lawyers – excel at a range of activities at work but don't necessarily enjoy all of them. I'm keen to understand what, if anything, brings joy.
- "What is their outstanding behavioural weakness at work on which you feel others would agree?"
- "What should they do with their careers to maximise their fulfilment at work – even if you think they might disagree with you?"
- "How can I help them in small ways?"

Usually, referees agree on my client's D-Liability and with uncanny similarity in wording. Typical client self-assessments with referee feedback in brackets include:

- "I don't suffer fools" [they bully].
- "I have very high standards" [they micro-manage, ferociously].
- "I can be very focused" [they never listen].

On the day before the Away Day, I ask new clients to send me an essay on their lives to date: "I was born on [date] ... in X location, of Y parents, with Z siblings; went to school A, university B (if any); and C was my first job." I ask them to set out all the ups and downs of their lives to date to the extent they feel comfortable communicating in this confidential essay. I read these the day before the Away Day. Often, I have cried having read some of the stories because of the pain that some have suffered. I feel privileged to read these moving personal accounts of mainly ordinary lives and some extraordinary ones. Over 20 years, I have read many essays – some as long as 40 pages, others as short as two. The average was about 10 pages. What surprised me was the consistently high quality and similarity of the writing – clear, short sentences; flowing, factual accounts of lives. The primary purpose of the essay is to help me to understand as soon as possible their formative years' decisions and context so that I can understand their D-Liability and help them take a new decision to inform their A-Asset. In addition, the essay saves me time understanding the career trajectory behind their *curriculum vitae* (CV) so that I can help them work on their career PSB plan ('personal PSB'). Above all, the essays put them in a reflective mood about themselves – for the first time, in many cases. For most, the process is positively cathartic, if not enjoyable.

On the Away Day, I start the session on their D-Liability because it's the most difficult issue to address. I tell them it's good to get it out of the way first. I remind them that, although many clients find my sessions therapeutic, I'm not a therapist; that I was in therapy myself and that I know the difference between what I do and what therapists do – for example, therapists would say much less and ask fewer questions than I, and would work with transference and projection, among other therapeutic models. If my clients cry, as many do, I wait a little and then ask them why – a therapist would use silence in a different way. I tell them that I am helping them to increase their EQ levels, which have over recent years become central to senior leadership development approaches. That said, I'm at pains to point out that they must feel psychologically safe and must take responsibility for how far they wish to go in discussing painful issues; and that while I will address these at a high level, they may wish to work on them with a therapist in parallel to my work with them. Many take me up on this offer and I put them in touch with good therapists I know – particularly *Gestalt* therapists, an approach I favour.

I encountered many – far too many – in-house lawyers who were bullied by their employer clients but who found a way in our sessions of reframing their relationships –with themselves first, and then with their employer clients.

The Away Day starts with a flipchart page showing a blank soft balance sheet. Usually, by lunchtime, the sheet is completed. I set myself a target of sorting the D-Liability within the first 90 minutes, by which time – usually – there's what I call the 'Aha!' moment of the session, when the client figures out their own core issue from a work and career perspective. For them, it's the highlight of the day. For me, it's a privilege and a delight, and is why I do what I do. My go-to 'Aha!' moment case study is the micro-managing CEO who understood the link between his formative years' decision not to trust anyone because it was then unsafe to do so and his micro-managing behaviour as a CEO. There were so many others – for example, the GC who connected with the origin of his people-pleasing behaviour at work and how he could make a new decision about saying no more often. Most 'Aha!' moments – unsurprisingly, given the type of people I encounter at the top of their field – are to do with confronting the connection between their formative years and why they feel so driven at work. Of the three emotional intelligence components on which I focus – empathy, self-awareness and the ability to meet needs productively – the latter is the issue that presents most frequently – particularly among lawyers, in-house and out. They struggle with the conflict between their need to take care of themselves and their need to excel at work, with which their identity is so entwined. Often, they have come from formative years contexts in which it was difficult to negotiate their needs productively. What is pleasing for me – and them – is that as soon as they see the connection, they are quicker than many clients in addressing the issue.

I encountered many – far too many – in-house lawyers who were bullied by their employer clients but who found a way in our sessions of reframing their relationships – with themselves first, and then with their employer clients. My experiences as a witness to these painful stories explain to some extent why I became involved in the movement to change the regulatory context in which in-house lawyers operate. I write about this later in the book. Not all clients were in a place to connect with their core formative years issue, and I didn't push it. Some clients said when we met that their childhoods were idyllic – "Eleven out of 10," they would say – but when I read their essays, they would describe experiences well short of an 11 score. For some, I would gently bring this to their attention. For others, I would let it go. An interesting group were those who were sent to boarding school around age seven. Although sent away at the age of 12, not seven, I knew about boarding schools, having spent six years in them myself. I would ask them if they were the bullies or the bullied; or whether they stood by or got by. The answers varied considerably. Some said unapologetically and somewhat defensively that it "made me the man I am"; others said that the experience was devastating; and some said that boarding school was better than home life. Based on their answers, I would seek to determine the extent to which they felt they were up for change and for working further on the experience. In all cases, though, I would point out that – irrespective of their analysis – I felt that sending a child away from home aged seven must surely have psychological consequences. It did in my case. By age 12, for example, the blight of shame – on which more later – was well established in my psyche and my years at boarding school consolidated it. I'm not saying that was everyone's experience; but I found later that shaming and fear of shame dominate business life and feature regularly in client experiences, particularly those of lawyers, in-house and out. It's an ever-present curse. Its origin is in formative years, but it is remedial – as Brené Brown, among others, reminds us in her excellent Ted Talks.[10]

9. Soft profit and loss account

This tool, which I developed to work alongside the soft balance sheet, sets out the three benefits from your work and the three costs of those benefits. Clients like this tool because it addresses their soft surplus or deficit – usually the latter – in a manner which helps them address it. A blank template looks like this:

Soft P&L

Soft revenue
A
B
C

Soft costs

D

E

F

Soft surplus (deficit)

Soft revenue, in descending order of importance to you – A, B and C – are the three intangibles you need from your work. Here are seven I hear frequently:

- autonomy;
- intellectual challenge;
- a team;
- variety;
- progression;
- making a difference; and
- approval.

Soft costs, in descending order of importance to you – D, E and F – are the three intangible costs you are willing to endure to achieve your soft revenue. Here are a few I hear frequently:

- Stress – how much?
- Travel – how much?
- Long hours – how many?
- A tough boss – how tough?

Are you in soft surplus or soft deficit now in your job? If you are in a soft deficit, is it because of problems on the revenue side or the cost side, or both? What combination of soft revenues and soft costs would create the right environment for a soft surplus for you? Your answer to that question will help you figure out your personal strategy to achieve your personal purpose. In my view, if you can achieve a soft surplus of 75% most of the time – that is, *Most Mondays*[11] – you are you are doing well.

Notes

1   Eckhart Tolle, *The Power of Now: A Guide to Spiritual Enlightenment*, Yellow Kite, 2001.
2   A structured form of therapy in which a person dramatises a personal problem or conflict.
3   Marshall Rosenberg, *Nonviolent Communication: A Language of Life*, 3rd edition, PuddleDancer Press, 2015.

4   Eckhart Tolle, *The Power of Now: A Guide to Spiritual Enlightenment*, Yellow Kite, 2001.

5   Thomas A Harris, *I'm OK, You're OK*, Pan Macmillan, 1986.

6   Eckhart Tolle, *The Power of Now: A Guide to Spiritual Enlightenment*, Yellow Kite, 2001.

7   Brené Brown, *Daring Greatly: How the Courage to Be Vulnerable Transforms the Way We Live, Love Parent and Lead*, Penguin Life, 2015.

8   Roger Jones, "The Family Dynamics We Grew Up with Shape How we Work", *Harvard Business Review*, 19 July 2016, https://hbr.org/2016/07/the-family-dynamics-we-grew-up-with-shape-how-we-work.

9   William Glasser, *Reality Therapy: A New Approach To Psychiatry*, Wildside Press, 1990.

10 Brené Brown, Ted Talks on shame: www.google.com/search?q=brene+brown+shame.

11 The title of my next book.

Chapter 2: Your career – how to manage the business of your in-house career

1. Introduction

Your career as an in-house lawyer is a business. You are selling your professional services to your employer client for cash and soft benefits. You are a business of one. All the art and science of business apply to you as much as they do to the largest business. I have developed a career management model for clients to use to manage their careers. The starting point for managing your career is to consider your career equity.

2. Your career equity

'Career equity' is a term that I use to capture the intersection between the core components of the status of your career at a point in time.

Your 'career equity arc' is a term I use to capture the trajectory of your career equity from where it is now to where you want it to be, say, in three years' time. I find three years a reasonable period to forecast

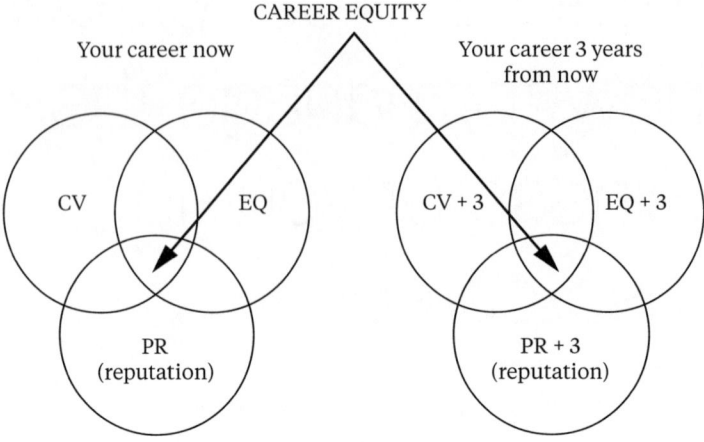

career objectives. The career equity arc helps clients to understand the link between their relationships and how they attend to them and their career success and fulfilment over manageable three-year intervals. How will your career equity look in three years' time? If you are, for example, deputy GC today, will you still be in that position three years from now? How will your CV have changed, if at all? Will you have changed or developed at all in respect of your self-awareness, empathy or ability to negotiate your needs productively – that is, your EQ? To what extent, if any, will your reputation – what I term your 'PR' – change over the next three years? Will people be saying the same things about you behind your back, good or bad, then as they are now? To what extent do you feel that you can control the arc of your career in respect of these three components over the next three years? To help you answer these questions, let's start with a detailed description of the three components of your career equity, starting with your CV.

2.1 Your CV

Your CV, or résumé, is a list of dates, organisations, titles and achievements and education – no more, no less. It's not an opportunity to declare that you are dynamic and thrusting (sic); nor is it a document that can be shaped for a particular role. It is what it is. I have written hundreds of these for clients over the years. I have read about the art and science of a great CV. There is no art. There is no science. A CV answers three questions, apart from your name and contact details:

- What did you achieve?
- Where?
- When?

That's it. The purpose of your CV – which means the course of your life – is to demonstrate, rather than assert, your competence to its readers, prospective employers, head-hunters and their keyword search databases by setting out in a simple list what you have achieved, where and when since you left primary school. It's not a document to be skewed, shaped or versioned for a particular role. It's not a pitch. Your cover letter is your pitch, and your CV supports that pitch. "I led a team of 10 people" is a sentence which demonstrates, potentially at least, your competence. The sentence "I am dynamic, inspirational and strategic" – whatever that means – is an assertion which demonstrates your incompetence in not understanding that the reader of your CV will never believe that you are dynamic, inspirational and strategic just because you say so. They are more likely to do so if they hear it from a referee or, perhaps, if you wrote: "I led a team of 50 people through a difficult merger process." For that reason, and in respect of the CVs I have written over many years for senior leaders finding new roles or launching portfolio careers, I always deleted the opening summary paragraph or pen portrait beloved by so many – especially those who say that they have not applied for a job in years. I acknowledge that opinion is divided on these introductory paragraphs. John Purkiss and Barbara Edlmair wrote in *How to be Headhunted*: "Many consultants and researchers ignore these pen portraits. Some even find them irritating...what they want from your CV is relevant factual information, not your opinion of yourself."[1]

I'm sure you will find other head-hunters who disagree. People like pen portraits because they are terrified of underselling. Yet these unnecessary paragraphs – often written by excellent leaders but without Tolstoyesque writing skills – are unnecessary at best and damaging at worst. Let your CV speak for itself and trust that the reader can make reasonable deductions from a simple list of dates (including months, with absolutely no gaps since leaving school or university) organisations, roles and a list of achievements, each on one line, starting with a strong verb – for example, 'launched', 'led', 'closed', 'integral to achieving' (if part of a team), 'developed', 'increased' and 'reduced'.

Although you might choose to provide a one-page summary CV and a longer, detailed version for head-hunters, most of my work is with senior leaders where the longlist for roles is usually short, so I would generally favour a two-page CV with a short one-page covering letter (but that approach is not appropriate in all circumstances). Your CV should include a summary of your education but not your interests, because you can't risk the reader's possible negative reaction or unconscious bias towards these.

2.2 Your EQ

EQ is a vast topic researched by many academics, notably Daniel Goleman.[2] I focus on three issues: empathy, self-awareness and your ability to have your needs met productively. Empathy is the ability to share someone else's feelings or experiences by imagining what it would be like to be in their situation. It is not to be confused with sympathy. You can be empathetic with someone but not sympathetic towards them. Many, although not all, leaders get to the top of organisations because they lack empathy. Their ruthlessness means they possess the so-called 'killer instinct' to push others aside in the service of their own ambition. They can take the tough decisions – code for being tough on others – without losing sleep. Being liked is not high on their agenda. People will work very hard for leaders with low empathy for fear of their wrath – a powerful incentive. But if a leader needs discretionary effort from them – meaning voluntarily going the extra mile – they won't get it. In a crisis, money can't buy the crucial and intangible discretionary effort required from a workforce which is essential for sustainable recovery. In a crisis, a leader is exposed much more nakedly than in normal times. They have no hiding place. In these circumstances, many double down on their ruthlessness and succeed for a while until their followers have had enough. Others flounder and fail because they cannot understand that one of the tools of surviving a crisis is the quality of leadership during that crisis.

Self-awareness means having good knowledge and judgement about yourself. In my work, I use a simple self-awareness test: I ask my leader clients whether they know what main behavioural weakness people in their organisation would say they have if I asked them to tell me – which I always do. If they don't know, there's a high chance that they frequently visit much unconscious pain on the people who work for them. They don't know what they don't know. Hubris – meaning excessive pride – is the bedfellow of low self-awareness; and hubris leads, ultimately, to failure – especially in a crisis. I find the ability to meet needs productively to be the most complex issue of the three EQ components in helping people to develop their emotional intelligence because getting one's needs met is at the heart of all conflict and all cooperation. Leaders with low empathy and self-awareness get their needs met through brute force. This approach is not productive over the long term in normal times and rarely in a crisis.

2.3 Your reputation

Your reputation – PR – is the consensus among other people about you which they express behind your back, and sometimes to your face. It is what it is. Do you know yours? Have you checked? Do you know how to change it even if you wanted to? When I ask clients these questions, a surprising number – to me at least – don't know what the reputational consensus of third parties is about them. Does it matter what others feel about you? Some people don't care. In a BBC documentary on former UK Prime Minister Theresa May, one of her close advisers said that what people don't understand about her is that she genuinely doesn't care whether anyone likes her or not. So many people do very well indeed by not caring about their reputation, but only up to a point. For most of us, however, we *must* care; and, indeed, at an ethical level, we *should* care. We live in a society and to function in it, we need to understand the impact we are having on it. In career terms, therefore, if you don't know what your reputation is, then it's in your interests to find out. It's easy: just ask enough colleagues what people say about you behind your back until you are clear on the consensus. Usually, you'll find they are saying something like, "You are great at X, Y and Z, but ..." What's your but? It will be behavioural, and you need to know. But you're not stuck with it unless you choose to stick yourself with it. By that I mean you can change your reputation by making small changes in your behaviour.

It is a source of great satisfaction to me in my work to witness clients make small changes in their behaviour, resulting in an unexpected and positive shift in their own reputation and in the behaviour of others. For example, one client, one day, stood up to their bullying boss in such an unexpectedly calm and clear way that their boss was taken aback and shifted their behaviour. Not a lot, but enough. That's all you need in behavioural change processes. Just enough to make a difference. However, reputation is not just about the bad stuff. It's also about what you are deemed to be good at or not good at by everyone else and how this language can be exaggerated, either way. For example: "He's *phenomenally* bright." Phenomenally? Really? Not just bright? Often, though not always, this is virtue signalling by the speaker keen to assert their expertise in judging who is phenomenally bright – meaning, by implication, that they are phenomenally bright themselves. If you have a reputation for being bright, then, rest assured, it's being overstated by others. For 'bright', you can substitute words such as *'strategic'*, *'inspirational'* and *'talented'* – provided, at all times, that these adjectives are accompanied by an over-the-top adverb: *'phenomenally'*, *'incredibly'*, *'hugely'*. Another example: "She's *hopeless* on her feet" – that is, a poor speaker. Hopeless? Really? Not remediable in any way? Just because someone is a nervous speaker or less confident on their feet than others doesn't mean that they are stuck with that fear. Stories about people overcoming their fear of public speaking are as ubiquitous as they are heart-warming. I used to get palpitations before speaking even in a small group and now happily – if not entirely free of nerves – speak to large audiences. It takes practice and encouragement from others. You are not your reputation unless you choose to be.

3. Your seven career options

Today – and on any day, because you must recommit daily to your career purpose if you are to feel fulfilled most of the time – you have seven career options. I have proposed these to new clients for as long as I have been in practice. I have offered a bottle of champagne to clients who can come up with a credible eighth. I have not given away a bottle of champagne since I chose Option 2 in August 2002. Some of the options are less relevant to in-house lawyers than to my clients who are not lawyers, but I set them all out here.

3.1 Option 1: Stay where you are

Your first option is to stay where you are and try to make your working life better. I meet many in-house lawyers who are desperate to leave their current job but shouldn't because they are not ready to leave. They should stay, try to make their working lives better by confronting the problems that will follow them wherever they go and then, and only then, should they leave. By 'make their working lives better', I mean reframing their relationship with themselves, the business of their career and their relationships with people they find difficult. They should experiment with new ways of working before they move elsewhere.

3.2 Option 2: Leave and launch a new business

Then, you have six leaving options. You can leave and set up your own consulting business in law or something else; or you can start a new business not connected with law. Many lawyers become entrepreneurs. However, if you take the consulting option, you must be able to market and sell your professional services consistently. Many people don't understand that working as an independent consultant can be a frustrating and financially insecure famine/feast experience. It takes time and commitment to build a reputation. You must be able to afford to take cash-flow risks. If you can't, don't choose that option. True consultants don't look at job advertisements. If you are consulting while looking for a new role, then be honest and say so on your LinkedIn profile. Launching a new consulting business in legal services or something else is, to be clear, a career change – from lawyer to entrepreneur – requiring a full understanding of the risks and opportunities of that transition. This option includes launching a portfolio career of NED roles. In-house lawyers can sometimes struggle to secure even one NED role, never mind a portfolio, because boards can feel they have ready access to legal skills. That said, some in-house lawyers who have the personality, experience and nous can build good portfolio careers. In 2016, I wrote a pamphlet titled *The Seven Deadly Sins of Nascent NEDs*,[3] because I helped many clients launch portfolio careers. I found that while they were all invariably bright, successful and experienced senior leaders, they didn't know what they didn't know about launching a portfolio career. They assumed it was their right and expectation to "pick up a few NED roles" because what got them to the top in corporate life would get them to the top in the NED world. They found it far harder than they expected to secure even one NED role.

3.3 Option 3: Leave and join a start-up
If you don't want to start your own business, you could join a start-up. If you join a start-up – no matter how well funded – as an in-house lawyer, make sure you do your due diligence on the founders and their backers regarding their ability and ethics, and ensure that they understand that you have an obligation to act with independence. I have witnessed many in-house lawyers struggle in start-ups because they are not allowed to do their jobs by inexperienced CEOs and those lacking a moral and ethical compass.

3.4 Option 4: Leave and join a growth business
If you want more job security but some of the excitement of a start-up, leave and join a rapid growth business. They are likely to be able to pay you more and tend to be more stable, although the independence and ethics points above apply equally to growth businesses. In addition, the executive boards of growth businesses – particularly those which have raised significant sums from private equity backers – tend to be under significant revenue pressure, which can translate into ethical pressure on legal teams.

3.5 Option 5: Leave and join a mature business
This is the classic option chosen by in-house lawyers. They move or are headhunted to well-established organisations where they may find more fulfilment – the same or worse than their previous organisation, depending on the culture of the organisation and of the legal function. Your due diligence on culture is key to a successful move to a mature organisation. Make sure you are not jumping from frying pan to fire.

3.6 Option 6: Leave and downshift

This option is open to very few people, but I include it because it is open to those who can afford to stop working altogether. If you can afford it, stop working if you like – at least in the accepted sense. Do things you love doing.

3.7 Option 7: Exploit family money or opportunities

Sometimes I meet people – admittedly few – who could work in their family's business or take advantage of family money or property. If you can, do consider it.

Whatever you decide, take full personal responsibility for your decision to stay and make it better; or to leave; or to accept that you don't have a choice. Above all, don't drift.

4. Your personal purpose, strategy and behaviour (PSB) plan

Clarity on your personal purpose as an in-house lawyer is key to achieving fulfilment in the business of your career. Three simple words: purpose, strategy and behaviour – PSB. Together, they are powerful. What is your PSB? The root cause of many relationship problems is that personal purpose remains unclear between the parties. The problem is that figuring out your PSB can be hard work, which is why so many people avoid the task. It can be a painful process if it forces you to confront issues about your life and career which are difficult to face. But it is worth the effort; and if you haven't figured out your PSB, I hope that this book will help you to do so.

4.1 Your career purpose (P)

What is your life about? Why are you a lawyer? What do you believe is the purpose of the legal profession? What is the purpose of the in-house function? A clear purpose can usually be expressed in one sentence. It is the foundation of strategy and behaviour in every situation. Your purpose (P), in career terms, is about why you do what you do. Is your purpose to make money, to make a difference, to be the best at what you do – or all three? Or something else? Or are you unclear, drifting or just getting by? The process of finding a purpose is a purpose, provided that there's a reasonable time limit on your reflections; so if you are searching for answers, then you have a purpose.

4.2 Your career strategy (S)

Your strategy is about how, in broad terms, you will achieve your career purpose as an in-house lawyer. 'Strategy' is one of the most abused words in the business dictionary. Some people think it's a plan. Others think it's behaviour. It's neither. A strategy describes how you will achieve an objective. How you manage your career path is a strategy, not a purpose. Your career goal may be to become a GC, but don't confuse that goal with your purpose. You may decide that adopting a strategy to work towards a GC role is likely to help you achieve your purpose of being what you can be, but it may not. You may be a brilliant and happy lawyer who loves practising law; but you may not be happy as a GC, which requires, primarily, a love of leading others and an ability to do so. You may neither love leading others nor have the ability to do so. The problem is that many brilliant lawyers are promoted to GC roles because they are brilliant lawyers and not because they are brilliant leaders. Moreover, many in-house lawyers feel they have failed if they have not yet made it to GC level, as if that were their career purpose. The system conflates role seniority with identity. You may find that your best strategy is to avoid promotion – even turn it down because you want to focus on practising law – perhaps by becoming an in-house topic expert.

4.3 Your career behaviour plan (B)

Your behaviour (B) embraces all your plans and approaches to implementing your strategy to achieve your purpose. It's your *modus operandi*. You may decide in advance to spend X years at Y business in Z role and then seek to move to a new role in another business or to stay in one organisation for your entire in-house career. Your decision will be subject to the frustrating constraint that movement at the top of your profession is limited. If your GC is settled into their role for the foreseeable future, and if your strategy is to achieve personal fulfilment by finding a GC role, then your behaviour plan must be to integrate an ongoing proactive GC job search into your daily life for many years, and not – as I hear frequently from clients – to wait for something "to come along" unless you are content in the meantime to accept your current role as a route to personal fulfilment in the moment. Acceptance of the moment, in mindfulness terms, is the key to peace and even joy at work. Acceptance is not the same as resignation. The nuance of acceptance is more like a willing surrender to reality than a resentful resignation. Your career behaviour plan is also about how you behave daily in the role you have now, how you fill it with meaning for you – even if it is less than what you want or need. Do what you do well because that is how you choose to live. Then go home and be fully present there too.

5. Your career-ism

Not long after Theresa May became UK prime minister, *The Observer* newspaper ran a piece encouraging her to define 'Mayism', lest she fall into the trap of being defined by others. I was pleased to see that a high-quality newspaper was ready to believe not only that she could have an -ism, but also that she could have it at the start of her term of office despite the arbitrary rules of -isms. Former Prime Minister Margaret Thatcher, owner of one of the most famous -isms, cuttingly said of her successor, John Major, that "there is no such thing as Majorism". Leaving aside the tone of the comment, it raised the question of who decides who should have an -ism. I'm interested because for some time, I have used the concept as part of my work with leaders. If I'm working with Joe Bloggs, I say: "What is Joe Bloggs-ism?" They ask: "What do you mean?" I sense that they feel that only famous politicians can have an -ism. My response is that there is only one you and, although you may be like other in-house lawyers, nobody can – to coin a questionable verb – in-house lawyer like you can. It reminds me of the famous quote from *Time* magazine when Pope John Paul II visited Canada. A man in the street said, "We have a Pope who knows how to Pope!" So, I ask you now what I ask my clients: "What defines how you lawyer as an in-house lawyer?" They usually respond by saying something like: "I don't know and, frankly, I don't see myself as very unique." I counter this with a point of grammar which may appear pedantic but isn't – you can't qualify the word 'unique'. You're unique or you're not. You can't be very unique. And since everyone is unique, you're unique. So what? The answer is: if you're unique, then the way you work is unique to you, whether you like it or not. Therefore, you have a choice: you can work with a conscious awareness of your uniqueness, or you can ignore the fact that you are unique and not bring the reality of your uniqueness into your awareness at work. What if you knew that you would feel more fulfilled at work by consciously accepting your unique behaviour as your unique -ism? Would it not be worthwhile to use it? Conversely, would it not constitute an opportunity cost to ignore it?

So, what is your -ism? It's about you, your purpose in life and how you live that purpose. If you take the time to clarify this and apply it daily, you and those around you will notice the difference. Start by making small changes in how you do what you do and see what happens. Your -ism is like a personal target operating model or your *modus operandi*. Most businesses have a target operating model. It usually has three elements: a market need; strategic resources; and processes by which the resources are applied to meet the market need. Likewise, your target operating model is about your needs, the resources you have at your disposal and the processes you use to deploy those resources to meet your needs.

But what if you don't know what you need; what if you are drifting or are driven by unclear drivers, some from your formative years? In that case, it might be useful to figure out what you need, not what you want. There's a difference. You may need to change your job because you drifted or were driven into it, but you may not want to do so. I acknowledge that this -ism approach sounds like hard work. It does because it is. Even the small changes required to shift your needle in a better direction are challenging. But the return on the effort invested is worthwhile. The reason Thatcherism made it into the history books and Majorism didn't was not because Major's leadership behaviour was worse than Thatcher's. It was because Thatcher – rightly or wrongly – was clear about what she wanted to achieve, and she articulated these objectives continually. I can't remember what Majorism was because Major didn't define it for us. That doesn't mean there was no Majorism. It was after all he, not she, for example, who was integral to the Irish peace process.

6. Managing your career arc

The quality of your career equity arc will depend on the extent to which you can make small changes towards improving your EQ. Changes to your CV and PR components will follow from changes to your EQ component. Specifically, that means increasing the extent to which you empathise with others, deepening your self-awareness and changing the way you get your needs met so that it becomes more productive for all involved. A small change in your levels of empathy might mean, for example, that in your interactions – especially with people who work for you – you include one question in each interaction which forces you to put yourself in their position. For example: "How are you?" "Does this make sense to you?" "What problems might this present to you?"

A small change in deepening your self-awareness might include counting to 10 mentally to give yourself time to check in more deeply than usual as to what you feel instead of acting, or reacting, on autopilot. Anger is a shallower emotion than, for example, anxiety. So, if you feel angry with someone at work, you may find that your deeper feeling is one of fear, humiliation or anxiety. So instead of shouting or shaming, you might start by saying, "I feel very concerned about the impact of X, Y, Z on me." Starting a sentence with, "I feel..." (see the discussion of Feel/Need/Do in Chapter 1) will curtail you from shaming others. Small changes in your behaviour brought about by deepening your self-awareness will impact the quality of the outcomes for your career and for your employer client organisation, especially in a crisis. If you start making small changes in how you get your needs met, you will find that that there will be a bigger impact on the outcomes than the effort you put into making those small changes. If you are a GC and if your usual style of getting your needs met is X, then I suggest that today you add a new component, Y, to your behaviour, where Y is a mental or verbal checking out whether you and the other person or persons have precisely the same shared purpose. Frequently in my work with leaders, I find that they become very frustrated with colleagues, only to find on deeper analysis through my one-to-ones with the legal team that their colleagues are looking at matters through completely different lenses than the GC. It takes only a few minutes to step back and set your request in the context of a shared organisational purpose; whereas days, weeks and months can be lost if you feel that one of your colleagues just doesn't 'get it'. It's not an 'it' that they don't get. It's you they don't get. And it's your responsibility, not theirs, to ensure everyone shares the PSB statement. Start making small changes in your behaviour today; for as Primo Levi wrote,[4] "If not now, when?" So, tell everyone where you are now as a GC and why, where you are going and how you're going to get there. Then you can claim your -ism.

7. How to sell yourself at interview, and your ideas and budget

One of the most important tools in your career toolbox is how to sell. Many years ago, my job brought me into contact briefly with Greg Dyke – then CEO of London Weekend Television (LWT) and later CEO of Pearson Television and subsequently, more famously, director general of the British Broadcasting Corporation. He is unlikely to recall my name, but I will never forget him because he was an exceptional leader and was famous for his one-liners about business and work. "Are you buying or selling?" he asked me on one occasion. Unusually for me, I was then buying television facilities at LWT. I've never forgotten that simple question. The statement behind the question is clear: in business, most of the time, you are either buying or selling – whether it is for goods or services or ideas or at interview or asking for a salary hike. Usually, I was selling – and so are you as an in-house lawyer, although not always. Yes, you will be a buyer of out-of-house services, but that's not necessarily onerous. More onerous is selling your ideas, your budget, your proposals to your employer client and to your colleagues; and winning at interviews against the competition. I have read many books on selling. My top two favourites are *You Can't Teach a Kid to Ride a Bike at a Seminar*[5] and *The Challenger Sale*.[6] The former is notable for its emphasis on how not to duck the hard questions in selling. My favourite question from the book is: "Are our conversations over?" I felt nervous the first time I used that question in an email to a potential client who was not responding to my emails. I was concerned that it might come across as too blunt. The feedback I received was that it does come across bluntly, but it works. The question invariably prompts people to resume the conversation; or if not, as happened on one occasion, they saved me time by saying that our conversations were indeed over for the moment. The second book was recommended to me by a law firm partner. It is excellent not only for professional services selling generally, but also for selling ideas and proposals within organisations, especially by in-house lawyers. The authors take a counterintuitive approach to selling. They argue that you should teach buyers about what you know about their needs based on your experiences with others; about your generic insight; about the generic cost and opportunity cost of their ignoring the issue; about an ideal generic solution. Then – and only then – should you present your specific solution. I have developed my own sales model, a synthesis of what I have read, and which I pass onto clients.

7.1 My selling approach

(a) Step 1: There's no sale without a need

Unless there's agreement about the need or pain of the buyer, explicit or latent, you can't sell anything – product, service, idea or yourself at an interview – to anyone. So, the first task in selling is to get the buyer to acknowledge their need; or, if they don't, the seller must persuade them to acknowledge a latent need. But implicit in Step 1 is an acknowledgement by the seller that it is their responsibility to sell and not the responsibility of the buyer to buy. I find that in-house lawyers can struggle with taking responsibility for selling their ideas, budgets, proposal, role and purpose to their employer clients. They are not alone. Politicians routinely make this error. If you are an interviewee, then you are selling. Your interviewer is buying. Grasp that and your chances of success will soar. Sadly, many – especially senior leaders – struggle to postpone attending to their own needs before addressing the needs of the buyer. The way to surface needs, explicit or latent, is to ask as many open biased questions necessary to establish beyond doubt the buyer's needs – as they see them, not as you see them. Open biased questions include: when? Where? Why? What? How? If a head-hunter is interviewing you, your task is to sell to them the reasons why they should include you on their shortlist. Head-hunters are buyers of first instance. So many interviews are lost by interviewees because they pitch to the head-hunter as if they are not the buyer in the first instance. That's fatal. You must discover what will make the head-hunter include you on the list and why they might exclude you from the list. Do not move to Step 2 until you are sure you know, accurately, the buyer's needs. You can test this by summarising the needs back to the buyer. If you get the summary right, the buyer will tell you directly and/or through their body language whether you are right. When you get verbal and/or physical confirmation – usually involuntary nods – that you have summarised their needs correctly, then, and only then, move to Step 2. I call these confirmations 'noddies'. If you don't get any noddies, do not move to Step 2 because you will make the cardinal error of pitching to the wrong needs and, as I have witnessed on so many occasions, you won't know what you won't know about why you are not called to the next interview. I find it painful witnessing bright, successful and able people, with little selling experience, bewildered when they hear that they have not been shortlisted.

(b) Step 2: Demonstrate, rather than assert
Benefits before features is a well-established rule in selling. You must have enough EQ to empathise with the nuanced needs of the buyer and then have the nous to sell in the benefits of your proposition first, not its features, in respect of needs by the buyer. Once you establish, accurately, the buyer's needs, you can move to Step 2 as follows. Taking each need, in turn, tell a story that demonstrates rather than asserts your ability to meet that need. When you have finished telling your story, ask the buyer if that story demonstrates that you could meet that need. If yes, move on to the next need and story. If not, ask in what way that story does not meet their need. Find the gap. Examples of assertion include: "People tell me I'm a visionary leader"; "I don't suffer fools"; and "There's very little in this sector I don't know." Examples of demonstration include: "If you call X, I believe they will say they felt well led by me – do you want their contact details?"; "An example of how I successfully motivated my team is when I involved them in X by doing A, B and C"; and "I'm pleased to say that I'm frequently asked to speak at conferences because I believe event organisers feel that I have deep knowledge of D, E and F. Last year, for example, I spoke X, Y and Z conferences." When you get to the end of the buyer's list of needs and finish your demonstration stories, there will be a gap between their

needs and your pitch. There is always a gap. Always. No one gets a score of 10. Ever. If you do, it's either a lie or a mistake. If you haven't found the gap, you can't move to Step 3. If you do, you will miss a trick. Most interviewees who fail do so because they are afraid to ask the gap question. Mind the gap.

(c) Step 3: Close the gap

The key to closing a sale is closing the gap between the needs of the buyer and their perception of your solution. If I'm selling to you, I will say: "If, on a scale of 0–10, where 10 means you're going ahead with the deal and 0 means you're not – where are we now on that scale?" The answer to this question is invariably: seven. A score less than that and you should wonder whether they are serious about buying at all. Next, I would say: "What does the gap of three represent to you? How can I persuade you to give me a 10? What's missing for you today?" If you can't close that gap, you can't close the sale. This technique is particularly useful at job interviews. I find some clients who I prepare for interview struggle with asking this question. They worry that it is too confrontational and could be misinterpreted as taking over the interview. That risk exists for sure, and you need to be sensitive as to how you phrase the question based on the personalities in the room; but I argue that if they have a problem with that reasonable question at interview, why would you want to work for them? A compelling reason to ask the question is that it works, based on my own experience in selling and on the experience of my clients. When I debrief clients after interview, I ask, "How did you get on?" Some say, "I don't know; it's hard to judge." Others say: "I asked your difficult question, and it works because I found out where I stood before I left the interview." Why would you leave an interview without at least trying to find out what they feel your chances are? It's Adult-Adult[7] behaviour to check out how you are doing in any selling situation. Interviewers are more likely to hire you if you're the least risky – not necessarily the best – candidate. Their incentive is in avoiding the reputational shame of being responsible for a 'poor hire'. Ironically, this fear leads invariably to poor recruitment processes. Having established, accurately, your buyer's needs and demonstrated, rather than asserted, your ability to meet those needs, and in doing so surfaced the gap between the buyer's objections and a deal, the next step is to close the gap. There is always a gap. If they say there isn't, they're lying. Here's how to close the gap using this imaginary dialogue:

You: As I understand it, you need A, B and C and I have, hopefully, demonstrated how I can meet those needs; so if 10 is I'm hired and zero is I'm not, where am I on that scale now, taking the other candidates into account?

Them: You're at about seven. *[They almost always say seven if you're in with a chance.]*

You: How do I close the gap between seven and 10? What about my pitch has you still concerned that I may not be the best on the list?

Them: Well, you say you have international experience, but you have only led one team outside of the UK and that was in Amsterdam. That's not precisely global leadership, is it? Other candidates have led teams on all five continents.

You: Oh. I see – so multi-country international experience is a deal-breaker then, is it?

Them: No, we knew the extent of your international experience from your CV, of course; but when it comes to deciding on a shortlist – it's tricky, because there's often just a cigarette paper between the finalists – and, you know, we must base our decision on something.

You: I see. So, you feel I could do the job despite my narrow international experience, which I acknowledge *[NB: always accept their take on you; don't push back unless they are factually wrong and to a material extent]*; which means that the other candidates with extensive global leadership experience may be weak in areas I'm strong. Is that fair? *[This is a 'closed question' – the answer is yes or no. Don't use these unless you know the answer in advance.]*

Them: Yes

You: So, if you could be persuaded that the risk associated with appointing me with my narrow international experience is less than the risk of appointing my nearest rival on the list with extensive international experience but weaker than me on other criteria, you would choose me?

Them: Potentially. There are other factors, of course …

You: Okay – so let me deal with the international experience issue first. What, for you *[an open question]*, is the most essential quality required of a global leader in your organisation?

Them: For us, it's about the ability to lead, motivate and manage a team remotely.

You: I understand. So, if I could demonstrate that I could learn to lead in that manner, my score would increase beyond seven?

Them: Well, potentially … *[That's code for 'definitely']*

You: Okay. Over three years in my last role, I managed high-volume supplier and client relationships – not dissimilar to managing teams, I hope you agree – across the world. We also had restricted travel budgets and an ESG agenda; and of course, everyone worked remotely during lockdown. In addition, if you call my former boss, she will confirm that I was thrown in at the deep end with these key relationships and learned quickly how to deal with the tricky issues associated with managing remote relationships online, which both sides can find very frustrating. *[You are now back into a demonstration loop because the need is clear.]* Is there anything else? *[Always ask another question before making a statement.]*

Them: No, that's our main concern.

You: Do you feel I have addressed your main concern enough to nudge my score above seven towards a 10? *[Closed question]*

Most job search failures or unsatisfactory outcomes were caused by only one issue: failure to understand that a job search is a sales and marketing process.

Them: Yes.

You: Is there anything else? *[Open question]*

Them: Well, there's always personality issues … *[This is a key issue. Do they like you or not?]*

You: What kind of personality are you looking for?

And, so, off you go around the open question/demonstration/closed question cycle. Over the years, clients who have been brave enough to use this process said that it works; but it does require courage. Obviously, you must read the room; and if you feel that a dim view will be taken of your taking such a proactive approach, then don't do it. If so, however, you should consider whether these are people you want to work with, if they can't operate on a high EQ basis at interview. Those of my clients who didn't ask the questions, for whatever reason, and who didn't make the shortlist never knew why not – unless, of course, I called the head-hunter to ask. Bizarrely, head-hunters would tell me the truth, knowing that I would tell my client. Frequently, they would give me different feedback from the feedback they gave my client.

8. Managing your job search

Since 2002, I have assisted in scores of executive and non-executive job searches across all sectors, from oil and gas through telecommunications, media and technology to legal services. I have found that most job search failures or unsatisfactory outcomes were caused by only one issue: *failure to understand that a job search is a sales and marketing process.* Most applicants – even sales and marketing professionals – are inexperienced at selling and marketing themselves. This problem would not be so acute if applicants would accept that they don't know what they don't know about sales and marketing. Lawyers are the worst offenders. One law firm equity partner once asked me: "What's all this fuss about marketing, eh? All one needs, surely, are 40 tickets to Wimbledon?" I answered in the negative.

Then use creative visualisation. Imagine signing your new contract and imagine your first day – the start of your first 100 days in your new role. Work backwards in your mind's eye through the various stages, connecting with these deeply. Is creative visualisation necessary? Does it work? It's necessary because it helps you connect with an unfamiliar process. It works for that reason. Imagine your job search process as a funnel: start at the wide end and finish with a job and your first 100 days at the narrow end. The funnel is about narrowing your approach as you proceed. It's about focus. You start with leads.

8.1 Leads

Leads are potential job opportunities. They come from two activities: your proactive job search process and your reactive job search process. Your proactive process is one in which you approach targets or find targets through networking on and offline. Your reactive process is driven by head-hunters and advertisements. You are not in control; they are. Your proactive job search refers to job search activities which you originate and control: researching target organisations that match your criteria; longlisting targets; shortlisting targets; researching main and operating board members and key decision makers; researching introductions to or direct approaches to target decision makers; arranging introductions or making direct approaches; arranging meetings; preparing your pitch for meetings and for follow-up meetings.

Allocate 70% of your energy to your proactive search. Don't worry if there are no apparent vacancies. Your approach to a target may prompt one. If it doesn't, your meeting may well lead to another introduction. Remember that you are a professional services firm on legs. All the art and science of marketing and selling professional services apply to you.

Your reactive job search is that proportion of your job search which is reactive to head-hunters and job advertisements. I call it reactive because you have no control over it. I recommend you allocate 30% of your energy to your reactive job search and de-risk it as follows: register with all the appropriate head-hunters, job boards and alerts. Make sure your CV contains the relevant keywords so that you will be found on their systems. Build personal relationships with head-hunters if you can. Understand their needs. Your first task is to get a meeting with them. Your second task is to persuade them to put you on their shortlist. At this stage, they are the gatekeeper. Focus on them, not their client. Make sure your cover letters start with the job needs, not with you. In other words, don't start your cover letter with 'I'. Be patient. The reactive process, if done properly, is hard work indeed – endless applications, emails and research. Many successful, otherwise very hardworking people who find themselves searching for a job are reluctant to put in the hours. It's a psychological reaction. I understand why. They resent having to do it. They feel angry. Especially those who've had a difficult exit from their last job. If you are in that bracket, spend some time grieving (don't laugh – it's a process) for your lost job, and commit to the fact that your job now is to find a job. Then work hard, but only 30%, on your reactive search because the process is almost a lottery. But hard work will maximise your chances. For sure.

8.2 Opportunities

Opportunities are leads which you have qualified in and have a percentage possibility of turning into a role: 10% qualified in; 25% first meeting; 50% interview process; 75% shortlist; 90% negotiation; and 100% job offer. Don't self-deceive on the percentages or overstate your 'irons in the fire', especially at the 10% stage. Be ruthlessly honest with yourself.

8.3 Your pipeline

Your pipeline = leads + opportunities. Keep it full, especially when you are on a shortlist. There's nothing more depressing in the process than being blindsided by an unexpected rejection only to find that your pipeline is empty.

8.4 Your covering letter

Many job opportunities are lost before a selection process is barely underway, sadly, because people forget that the purpose of a CV and a covering letter is to secure a meeting, not a job. Your covering letter, not your CV, is the bespoke part of your pitch. Its purpose is to explain to the reader in summary why they should interview you, not why they should hire you. You are selling the benefit to them of meeting you. Don't try to the win the job at this stage. Win a meeting. This is particularly important if the first meeting is with a head-hunter. You need to close them, before you close the sale with their client. To close them, you need to understand their need. Their need is to collect a fee as soon as possible, to maintain a good relationship with their client mainly by delivering a successful search process, and to keep you onside, now and in the future, in case you could become a client. Remember: you are not their client.

So, start your cover letter by setting out briefly your understanding of the need of the hiring organisation – as in: "I'm writing to apply for X, as set out in Y, and I understand that you are looking for D, E and F." Then briefly set out the key points as to why you meet that need, ensuring that there is evidence for each of these points in your CV and drawing attention to those points – as in: "I believe I meet your needs E and F because, as you can see from my CV, I have extensive experience of A and B; and while I have less of C, I feel I can come up to speed quickly on that area and my referees would, I believe, confirm my ability to do so." When trying to attract a head-hunter's attention, you need to demonstrate rather than assert why they should bother keeping you on their radar. To demonstrate that I practise what I preach, my CV is set out[8] on my website. It includes annotations in italics as to my feelings and motivations. I'm not suggesting you include these in your CV, but you may find them interesting as they reveal what I suspect many readers wish from a CV but never get. That's why there is no such thing as a perfect CV. It is what it is: a list which invites questions as to who you are, where you are now and why; your purpose in life, your strategy to achieve that purpose and your plan, if you have one to implement that strategy. It about your uniqueness. It's about you. Your -ism.

8.5 The interview process

The interview process usually consists of a first interview, second and further interviews leading to a final interview, followed by an offer or a rejection.

8.6 Due diligence, contract negotiation and whether to accept long-term incentive plans

If you receive a job offer, the temptation to avoid the due diligence step is great because of the relief that your search appears to be finished. But don't skip the due diligence step. On one occasion, a client who received a job offer admitted to me that he felt very uncomfortable with one member of the senior leadership team. We carried out due diligence on that member, after which my client decided – reluctantly, but rightly – to reject the offer. Regarding contract negotiation, there is little advice I can give in-house lawyers, save to say that you should keep relationship issues firmly in mind as you negotiate your employment contract. You may win contract points in the contract but lose relationship points, and you won't know. Your job search is not over, in my view, until you have survived your first 100 days – see Chapter 3. Meanwhile, use the steps below to manage your job search.

First, a word on long-term incentive plans (LTIPs) and bonuses: you may want to consider waiving your LTIPS and bonus plans in return for higher salary on the grounds that these might be perceived as compromising your independence. Only three lawyers of the hundreds I know have done this and they found that it made a difference to how they were viewed at meetings. I'm not saying that you cannot act with independence and retain LTIPs. I'm saying that it's an issue of perception of which you should be aware, and you should make a conscious choice and take responsibility for that choice.

9. Your seven-step job search plan

9.1 Step 1: Start with humility

"I tick all the boxes", many clients tell me. "No, you don't," I reply. No one ticks all the boxes. Your targets don't even know all the boxes they want ticked. Sometimes they make them up as they go along; or they can't say what they are because they are illegal (eg, race, sex, age, religion); or they have an unconscious (or conscious) bias against you for whatever reason. So, know that you don't know what you don't know about 'the boxes' and remember: looking for a job is a full-time job and is different from any job you have done. If you can't do it full time, accept that downside.

9.2 Step 2: Draft a word-perfect personal purpose (P)

"I must keep my options open," many clients tell me. "You must not," I say. The opposite. You must narrow your options. Focus is key. Write a word-perfect purpose statement on your chosen option. That's a hard statement to craft. Give it time.

9.3 Step 3: Stick to one strategy (S)

"I've decided to 'go plural'", a client said to me, meaning they had decided to launch a portfolio career consisting of non-executive directorships, consulting and pro bono work. "Great," I said. "So that means you won't be looking at job adverts then, yeah?" "Well," they said, "If the right thing were to 'come along', no." That's two strategies. Neither will succeed, fully. You wouldn't tolerate two strategies at work, so why tolerate it in the business of your career? Jobs are like Godot. You wait for them to come along in vain.

9.4 Step 4: Decide on your job search behaviour (B)

Decide how you will behave during your job search, whether you are writing a covering letter, networking or at an interview. What impression do you want to give which reflects you? Stick to your behaviour plan. The market has a gimlet eye for behavioural inconsistencies. It takes pleasure in catching people out.

9.5 Step 5: (Re)Learn the art of marketing

Since your career is a unique professional services business, all the art and science of marketing apply to you. Use them. Learn or relearn the four Ps[9] of classic marketing: product (service), price, place, promotion. What are you selling? How much do you cost? Where will you deliver your services? How will you promote yourself?

9.6 Step 6: (Re)Learn how to sell yourself (see section 7 above)

There are three questions for you in selling during a job search:
- What does the buyer organisation need and why?

- Can you demonstrate, rather than assert, that you can meet that need?
- Can you close the gap between the buyer's objections and a deal?

9.7 Step 7: (Re)Learn how to buy

When you know you have closed the deal at interview, start buying. The fancy term for this step is 'due diligence'. This is a difficult step because you want it to work out and the relief of getting over the line can blind you to the need to check that the job is likely to work out for you. So many clients say in their first 100 days that their new job is not working out. You should avoid this at all costs. Sometimes it's impossible to find out and you must take the risk, but listen to your gut. Better that than find yourself back on the job trail within a year.

Notes

1   John Purkiss and Barbara Edlmair, *How to be Headhunted: The Insider's Guide to Making Executive Search Work for You*, How to Books, 2005.
2   Daniel Goleman, *Emotional Intelligence: Why It Can Matter More Than IQ*, Bantam Books, 1995.
3   Ciarán Fenton, *The Seven Deadly Sins of Nascent NEDs*, Oaktree Press, 2016.
4   Primo Levi, *If Not Now, When?*, Michael Joseph Ltd, 1986.
5   David H Sandler, *You Can't Teach a Kid to Ride a Bike at a Seminar*, Bay Head, 1996.
6   Mathew Dixon and Brent Adamson, *The Challenger Sale: How to Take Control of the Customer Conversation*, Portfolio/Penguin, 2012.
7   Thomas A Harris, *I'm OK, You're OK*, Pan Macmillan, 1986.
8   www.ciaranfenton.com/about.
9   Philip Kotler, *Marketing Insights from A to Z: 80 Concepts Every Manager Needs to Know*, John Wiley & Sons, 2003.

The practice of law in-house is your core business. The success of your practice depends on the quality of your relationships. The quality of your relationships is a function of your investment in them.

Chapter 3: How to manage your relationships at work as an in-house lawyer

1. Introduction

This chapter is about applying the tools, principles and models above in your day-to-day practice of law in-house. How you apply these will depend on the decisions you have taken regarding your personal PSB, your assessment of the PSB of your employer client (employer client PSB) and how those two PSBs are interdependent for you. The more time you invest in these foundational steps, the more return you will receive in personal growth, fulfilment and success – whatever you decide success means to you. From this strong personal foundation, you will do your best work for your employer client, for its stakeholders and for society. You will approach your practice of law in-house consciously and not unconsciously. Your application of the tools in your relationships will be mindful. In the dysfunctional world you operate in, mindfulness is your ally, unconscious behaviour your enemy.

The practice of law in-house is your core business. The success of your practice depends on the quality of your relationships. The quality of your relationships is a function of your investment in them. To this end, I have developed a relationship grid (see below) which I have used not only with CEOs, NEDs, other directors and GCs but also those starting their careers or in mid-career. In-house lawyers at all stages of their careers have used my relationship grid concept and associated tools for many years. Some create a grid on paper or a spreadsheet; many do it in their heads. The aspect of the grid that grabs their attention most is applying a red, amber or green (RAG) status to each of their relationships. This is because they are familiar with the RAG system on their risk registers. They see the relationship grid as a personal risk register. In this chapter, I describe the grid and what to do when your relationships go from green to amber or red. Problems include conflicts within the legal team; conflicts with the organisation that impact on all parties; conflicts between the legal function and the executive or main board; and independence issues. In this chapter, I also set out how you might approach the first 100 days of a new role.

In respect of relationships, you may find this quote from the Mental Health Foundation useful:

> Relationships are one of the most important aspects of our lives, yet we can often forget just how crucial our connections with others are for our physical and mental health and wellbeing.

> People who are more socially connected to family, friends, or their community are happier, physically healthier, and live longer, with fewer mental health problems than people who are less well connected.

> It's not just the number of friends you have, and it's not whether or not you're in a committed relationship, but the quality of your close relationships that matters. Living in conflict or within a toxic relationship is more damaging than being alone.

> As a society and as individuals, we must urgently prioritise investing in building and maintaining good relationships and tackling the

barriers to forming them. Failing to do so is equivalent to turning a blind eye to the impact of smoking and obesity on our health and wellbeing.[1]

2. Your first 100 days

Your first 100 days in a new role are special because you can't – obviously, but not always remembered – have a second first 100 days in the same role. These are unique days. They start with hopes and fears. You hope that all will be well and so do they. By 'they', I mean the people who hired you. They will be as nervous as you are. You will fear that you've made a mistake and so will they. But the bigger burden is on you. The view formed of you by others, the quality of those early relationships formed and your reputation generally will, by the end of the 100 days, be difficult to change by you. You will make irrevocable first impressions in your first key email, first meeting, first follow-up actions and especially in your first decision. The good news is that you will have a clean sheet to write a new chapter in your career, in your life and in theirs.

You will have a fresh opportunity to present whatever face you choose. You can decide what of your previous behaviour you will continue, what you will stop and what new behaviour you will try to adopt. Spend time reviewing the highlights and lowlights of your previous role. What went well and why? What, if you had the time back again, would you do differently? It reminds me of when I changed schools at age 15. I had been very unhappy at my previous school. I was young and socially immature for my age. I had no guidance day to day in a boarding school in which thuggery and kindness were present in equal measure. The new school was bigger and a better environment for me, but the key change for me was to start afresh as I meant to continue.

Remember that they – the jury – will stay out for variable lengths of time. I have facilitated scores of first 100 days programmes. I find that, on average, you will probably encounter your first amber or red relationship by Day 15. On one occasion, a client who had just started a new role as chief operating officer (COO) encountered a red

When the jury comes in on your first 100 days, you're stuck with their decision. It will be impossible to lodge an appeal. So, make the best of this honeymoon period.

relationship in his grid by Day 5 because a decision which was taken before he arrived caused a serious risk event in his first week and was now his responsibility. He said that, since he didn't know his colleagues or the politics of the relationships between them, he felt stuck as to how best to proceed, whom to trust and to whom he should give a wide berth. I suggested he ask his CEO to advise him how to proceed and with whom. But could he trust his CEO? Well, if he couldn't, it seemed to me, he shouldn't have taken the job in the first place. He got through the problem. It struck me at the time, and since, the extent to which senior people can feel alone among colleagues. Sometimes this is unavoidable but often people are afraid to take the risk of asking for help from colleagues for fear of being rejected by them or showing weakness. It's worth the risk. As one therapist said to me: "If someone rejects you, it's a statement about them, not about you." But you may be pleasantly surprised to find that others are happy to help you, not least because they feel alone themselves. So be prepared to encounter troublesome relationships and to take risks from Day 1. When the jury comes in on your first 100 days, you're stuck with their decision. It will be impossible to lodge an appeal. So, make the best of this honeymoon period. Here are seven steps to reduce risks and maximise your opportunities in your first 100 days:

- **Step 1:** Be clear on your personal purpose in life and at work before Day 1. If you're not, you will be in trouble before you start and you won't know why. Your new colleagues will be quick to project an assumed and often erroneous purpose onto you if you don't get in there first with yours.
- **Step 2:** Listen 70% of the time. Ask lots of open biased questions: who? What? When? Where? How? By 'biased', I mean biased towards surfacing information that will help you populate your relationship grid.
- **Step 3:** Demonstrate through your actions – don't assert – how your personal purpose links to the purpose of the legal function within the organisation and to the purpose of the organisation – assuming that the latter is clear, which it often isn't. Do your best. The interdependence of these purposes will make or break your first 100 days.
- **Step 4:** Communicate clearly what you intend to deliver in your

first 100 days and make sure you under-promise and over-deliver.

- **Step 5:** Take this unique opportunity to make small changes in your behaviour based on your review of your last role.
- **Step 6:** Never send a material email or text before you speak to the recipient. Never. Ever. You're not Tolstoy. Your former colleagues might have come to tolerate your telegraphic/florid/bland writing style over the years. Your new colleagues won't.
- **Step 7:** When you encounter your first amber or red relationship, work through your feelings, your needs in relation to those feelings and your options on how to handle the amber or red – ideally with a third party (see Feel/Need/Do in Chapter 1). How you deal with your first amber/red encounter will define your reputation and your first 100 days. Your new colleagues will judge you more on how you dealt with your relationships and less on what you delivered. Your character will be judged on how others felt when you interacted with them.

In extremis, you can decide to leave your new job at the end of your first 100 days without too much damage. We all make mistakes. Better to take that tough decision then when the market will understand. Otherwise, and ideally, you should stay at least two years in a role or risk losing credibility in the job market. An even tougher decision is for your new employer to accept that they made a mistake in hiring you and ask you to leave before the end of your first 100 days. This is rare. I find that more hiring mistakes are made by hirers than by applicants. How many people in your organisation do you feel were poor hiring decisions? Why? Your answer will be as much a statement about you as about them.

3. Your relationship grid

Relationship	What's their PSB?	What constitutes success or failure in your relationship with them?	Today, is that relationship red, amber or green?	Remedial actions? Getting back to green
Me				
Family 1				
Family 2				
Other ...				
My employer client				
My boss				
Colleague 1 ...				
Colleague 2 ...				
Report 1				
Report 2 ...				
External adviser 1 ...				
Other 2 ...				
My regulator				
The environment				
Society				

The relationship grid is a tool I developed, initially to help my clients – lawyers or not – who signed up for my First 100 Days Programme to avoid red relationships in those critical days. They then found that the grid is useful at any time. Here are the steps to populating your relationship grid. In the first column, list your key relationships, starting with yourself, then your family – a line each for each person in your family by name. But not just 'my family' – then followed by your employer client; your boss (ie, your line manager); your peers, by name; your team members, if you have a team – again by name; key clients or stakeholders – until you feel you have covered every key relationship. In Column 2, reflect on their PSB. If you don't know it, ask them. What do they need? Put yourself in their shoes. Understand their perspectives. They may not know it themselves. Perhaps you can help them – or at least, you can find out the extent to which they are acting unconsciously or not. This insight will help you to manage, navigate or deal with those relationships more effectively – whatever verb you favour, provided that you use a verb and not the term 'relationship management', which borders on management-speak and distances you from the mindful task of taking great care in how you relate to others.

You can now RAG each relationship as you see it. You feel in red with X, but you think they feel in green towards you. Why? You feel in red with Y and you know that the feeling is mutual. What are you going to do about this? You feel in green with Z, but you feel they're in amber with you. Why? Why is your relationship with your partner at home in amber, if not red? Teams and boards, like families, fight all the time. The job of a leader is to create an environment in which everyone thrives. There was a time when playing one member off against another through a divide-and-rule strategy was considered the norm. No longer. Leaders must now lead using high levels of EQ and expect high EQ from board and team members.

4. Green relationships

Green relationships are those relationships on your grid which you can rate as good. They are going well – not just from your perspective, but also from the other party's perspective. By that, I mean you know that the other party in your relationship feels the same way about you as you do about them. You know this is true because you have checked it out with them. This checking-out process is important because some people make assumptions about others and are shocked if they find that their assumptions are incorrect – as I have found when I facilitate boards, executive boards and senior leadership team off-sites. "I never knew you felt that about me" are words you should never, ideally, hear yourself say, because it means your relationship is not clear. It means you have been flying blind. The process of clarifying and maintaining good relationships is hard work. It takes effort. It involves risk. It involves making yourself vulnerable. "Are we good?" is a shorthand phrase – often used in North America – that captures the mutual feeling that all is good between two people. Ask it. Use whatever words work for you. The answer you receive may be "No," which may shock you; but at least you will know. A good relationship is one in which both parties are clear about the other's purpose; clear about the strategy they are using to achieve that purpose and the behaviour plan they are using to implement their strategy to achieve their purpose; clear about each other's PSB. A good relationship is one in which there is mutual empathy, evident self-awareness on both sides and – critically – where it is possible for you both to articulate your needs clearly to the other person and either have them met or, if not, that you understand why that is not possible. I find in-house lawyers struggle with negotiating their needs. The problem stems from a reluctance to express feelings – indeed, to connect with them internally in the first instance. If that is your experience, then you may find – as others have found – that the Feel/Need/Do tool set out earlier in Chapter 1 can help you break through this block. Try this: in this moment, in relation to that other person in your relationship grid – family member, boss, colleague, whether they report to you or not, employer client executive, outside adviser – connect with what you feel about them right now; what you need in relation to that feeling and the options you have in communicating your feelings and needs in order that they can be met. Make sure you review the entire range of options – from sending an angry text to arranging a meeting to sort it out. Don't take your green relationships for granted. Feed and nourish them with attention. It is tempting to focus your emotional energy on your amber and red relationships to the exclusion of your green relationships. These can turn amber or red in an instant. The best way to maintain good relationships is to ask regularly and unprompted: "What do you feel? How are things? Are you okay? What do you need? Can I help?" Or words that feel comfortable to you. You might feel uncomfortable with this degree of emotional transparency. My advice is, as our children say, to suck it up. Feel the discomfort and do it anyway. These people can help you with your ambers and reds, and you theirs. It's about the power of kindness – a subject that, most probably, was not on your law school syllabus.

5. Amber relationships

Amber relationships are those that are in danger of turning red imminently – just like amber traffic lights, which change quickly (sometimes too quickly) to red. I spend much of my time in my board, executive board and senior leadership team programmes facilitating soft contracts between members whose relationships are amber. They are characterised by not being termed good. A board member will say, "I have a good relationship with X, but Y is tricky, or difficult," or this or that. You have amber relationships. So have I. We all do. We use various terms to describe them, but we don't describe them as good. The quality of the amber relationship is determined by the extent to which the parties are aware of the part they play in the relationship. Some people say of a relationship: "We rub each other up the wrong way." This is an indication of their acknowledgement of the part they play in the difficulties they experience in the relationship. This evidence of self-awareness indicates high levels of EQ. On the other hand, other people place the burden of responsibility for the relationship on the other party: "They are tricky"; "She's a nightmare"; "He's a bully." He may well be a bully – but that doesn't mean that you don't have a responsibility to manage your contribution to the health, or indeed the existence, of your relationship with him. We will deal with bullies, and ask if you are one, later. Meanwhile, the key point with amber relationships is the speed at which you need to convert them to green, or at least prevent them from turning red. Dealing promptly with amber and red relationships in the first 100 days of a new role is especially important. If you are a GC or lead a legal team, you can help your team members manage their relationship grids. Sometimes you may have to live with an amber relationship despite your best efforts to turn it green. My mother would have called this "pulling and dragging" with people – meaning doing your best. That's all you can do.

6. Red relationships

Red relationships are those in serious trouble. I don't mean ongoing difficult relationships. I mean relationships in danger of breaking down completely. These are dangerous for everyone – for you; for the other party; for your employer client; and ultimately for society. You can forget personal and organisational growth and success if you and/or the organisation tolerate or indeed promote red relationships. These are rightly called toxic cultures. They can't sustain. They may do so for some time; but sooner or later, the toxic cultures will create perfect environments for what you lawyers call serious existential risk events. These cultures choke off discretionary effort. No organisation can survive without that sort of effort. You will, however, regularly encounter red relationships that can be steered back to amber – or even green – if you follow simple rules: dig deep to understand what you and the other party feels; what you and they need in relation to these feelings; and what options you both have to negotiate meeting your respective needs. If that does not work – even with external facilitation – then you may need to part. Usually for in-house lawyers, this may mean *in extremis* you have to leave and find what you need elsewhere. However, most red relationships are remedial with effort and conversations – not emails, texts and passive-aggressive posts on social media.

Once, I was working with a board, two members of which were at war with each other. Their feud was known throughout the business. Everyone I spoke to said they hated each other. Since my mandate was to help improve 'engagement' throughout the organisation and this conduct at the top was not conducive to modelling best behaviour in the organisation, I proposed that I facilitate a meeting between them to help sort it out. At the meeting, I asked each to explain to me their complaint of the other. The first party indicated that they felt outraged,

Even when there are forceful resistors of change on a board or team, a shift in behaviour is possible if the other members of the board come together and support each other.

exposed and let down by the fact that the second party had not supported them at board meetings on issues that they had both discussed and agreed on outside of those board meetings. The second party – who had only joined the organisation the previous year from abroad and had no local business contacts – indicated that they were outraged, frustrated and let down by the first party because they never shared business contacts, even though they were in adjacent business lines. I asked them if there was anything else. They said no. I said that it seemed to me, based on the facts (and assuming they had told me the full story, which I suspected they hadn't – not least the reasons for their underlying mutual animosity) that their rift was remediable – at least to the extent of meeting each other's needs, if they could agree on a soft contract[2] as follows. First, both parties would meet before board meetings and agree on which issues they would openly support each other with at those meetings; and in relation to business development contacts, the first party would proactively share contacts when they could. Sounds simple. It was. They huffily agreed on the soft contract and, from memory, we may have discussed (as I do usually) how they might legislate for the breach of their contract. That is: how would they call each other out? Call? Meet? Go for a drink? The success of these contracts varies. Sometimes a soft contracting process with a full board can be pleasingly transformational – a word I rarely use. I'm not sure how successful the soft contracts were in this case, but I know that something shifted. And sometimes even a small shift in behaviour can sow the seeds of big change. Sometimes the unthinkable happens in relationships. For example, who would have thought that Ian Paisley and Martin McGuinness – the 'Chuckle Brothers'[3] – would become friends? Or that Nelson Mandela and FW de Klerk would agree on ending apartheid in South Africa? The success of these facilitations of red and amber relationships depends on the ratio of resistors on the board or team. The 10/20/70 rule[4] of change applies.

7. The 10/20/70 rule of change

I learned this rule when I started my first job as a managing director tasked with turning around a small division of a large organisation in terms of sales and operations which suffered from significant behaviour issues. I was young and inexperienced, and focused my energy on the resistors of change. My approach didn't work. In fact, I made things worse. Engaging with the resistors created, as one of my bosses liked to say, more heat than light. I sought the help of a boutique change consultancy. I wish I could remember which one; but among their models and tools, they recommended the 10/20/70 rule of change: 10% are stars – celebrate them (which I did); 20% are resistors – ignore or sack them (which I also did); and 70% are on the fence – woo them (which I worked hard at doing and managed to turn the division around). 'Woo' is a great word. It means 'entice' and to take responsibility for enticing. So, my soft contracting facilitations with boards and teams have worked best on boards where the number of resistors to change is low. However, even when there are forceful resistors of change on a board or team, a shift in behaviour is possible if the other members of the board come together and support each other.

8. Emails, texts and posts

What do you do when an email, text, post, tweet, remark – or the absence of one – upsets you at work?

> *What did he mean in paragraph three by, "Having said that …"? Did he mean what he said in paragraph two or not? Why did he copy Y? Who did he bcc? What if he bcc'd X and Z? What did she mean by "but" in that text? 'But' what? There shouldn't be a 'but'. There's no 'but'. What's she implying? I've done nothing wrong. I don't have the budget. She knows that. That's the last time I'm liking their tweets/posts. He always likes other people's stuff with lots of 100% – loads of 'Love Its,' links, 'supers' and emojis. He rarely likes mine. Makes me sick. It's been at least two hours since I sent that email/text/post/tweet and still no reply. No likes. No shares. What's going on? That's odd. Maybe I shouldn't have sent it …*

And on it goes.

I spend much of my time with clients helping them to manage their reactions to other people's communications. To be fair, not all communications are like those. But those are the communications that cause most pain. I'm no better than my clients. I get wound up too. I've spent hours awake worried about some emails and texts. But the key to managing relationships better is to relate better – note the verb. You can't relate best via emails, texts and social media posts. You are not Tolstoy. Neither am I. Once you press 'send', you have no control over how your text is interpreted at the other end. You think you have made yourself clear; but it's impossible for all but the best writers to convey accurately what they feel and need, and the possible actions required. Pick up the phone, Zoom or – better still – meet with the other party. Often clients send me draft emails they were about to send their boss or colleagues. Their draft emails are usually packed with rage but no call to action; no inquiry as to what was happening on the other side; and, critically, no thought to how their boss might react to the email.

9. Learn from Lincoln: don't send that email in anger

In his biography of Abraham Lincoln – *Lincoln*[5] – David Herbert Donald describes Lincoln's fury at General Meade's failure to prevent General Lee's escape into Virginia. Fear fuelled the president's anger. Modern CEOs and leaders, including GCs, will recognise this deeper feeling of fear beneath their anger if they take time to pause, stay in the present moment mindfully and acknowledge that anger is a much shallower feeling than the deeper silent screams of frustration and fear. Lincoln had much to fear after so many lost battles. The union's surprising triumphs at Gettysburg and Vicksburg in July 1863 led him to believe that they could end the war if only General Meade were to "complete his work". That's the modern equivalent of: "Just do it!" However, General Meade didn't 'deliver'. Lee's army escaped across the Potomac at Williamsport, Maryland into Virginia. There was a Cabinet meeting that day. And were that a crisis board meeting in today's terms, it would be said that the atmosphere was tense, to put it mildly. According to Doris Kearns Goodwin's description of the meeting in her *Team of Rivals*[6] – one of several excellent books on the president – Lincoln's face clearly revealed that he was "disturbed [and] disconcerted". That's 1860s code for: he was apoplectic with rage. "If I had gone up there, I

The language of business influences behaviour. It's easier to talk about employee engagement, diversity and sustainability – all nouns – than to talk about listening to understand, appreciating difference in hiring decisions, creating sustainable organisations – all sentences with verbs.

could have whipped him myself," he said. How many times do we hear CEOs exclaim: "Do I have to do it myself?" Lincoln understood the importance of clarity of purpose and how it drives strategy. After that Cabinet meeting, he wrote the equivalent of a stinking email to General Meade, described by Goodwin:

> *While expressing his profound gratitude for "the magnificent success" at Gettysburg, he acknowledged that he was "distressed immeasurably" by "the magnitude of the misfortune involved in Lee's escape. He was within your easy grasp, and to have closed upon him would, in connection with other late successes, have ended the war".[7]*

But he never sent the letter because, as Goodwin writes, "Lincoln held back, as he often did, when he was upset or angry, waiting for his emotions to settle."[8] That was a good decision and demonstrated Lincoln's high levels of EQ, because when he had calmed down, he was able to empathise with Meade, who had been in command for only four days before the Battle of Gettysburg and had experienced enormous losses there, was exhausted and in a state of great "mental anxiety". Lincoln came to appreciate, with the benefit of hindsight, that he had asked too much of Meade. Had he sent the letter, Meade – the hero of Gettysburg – would have been unreasonably traduced. So, emulate Lincoln: don't send that email in anger.

10. Your use of language

'Behaviour' is a plural noun; and although the word 'behaviours' has become common in business, I believe that for the purposes of behaviour change, the plural noun is better. This is not a semantic point. The language of business influences behaviour. It's easier to talk about employee engagement, diversity and sustainability – all nouns – than to talk about listening to understand, appreciating difference in hiring decisions, creating sustainable organisations – all sentences with verbs. These are examples of business attempting to dehumanise, categorise and distance itself from feelings, needs and actions required to meet them. You, with your training in the precise use of language, can be an agent of change in helping your employer client to reduce management-speak, with its imprecise generalisations and distancing nouns, which hinders personal and organisational growth and good outcomes for society.

For example, 'conduct' is a word that you could take a lead on in your organisation by using the full form of its definition – behaviour over time – on all occasions, rather using the noun on its own. Evidence of its hijacking into management-speak exists in the financial services sector in the aftermath of the Global Financial Crash in 2008, caused by unethical behaviour over time by those with power across the globe in that sector. When the dust settled, the word 'conduct' became ubiquitous in the financial services sector. Regulators, rightly, wanted to regulate behaviour; but they emphasised the word 'conduct' instead of the phrase 'behaviour over time'. In the United Kingdom, the Financial Conduct Authority was set up in 2013. There's a clue in its name as to its purpose. But many might argue that its strategy and behaviour – often very expensive box-ticking exercises – failed to address the systemic issues since the Banking Standards Board annual reports note that there has been little change in behaviour since the financial crash.

11. Managing upwards

I attended a leadership training programme in the early 1990s given by a consultant from Dynargie Group. The model that sticks out for me from that programme – because it works and is one that I pass on to clients – is a tool on how to manage upwards. If you are updating your boss, start with Results (R) – whatever constitutes a result for your boss. Tell it as it is. Don't bluff. Don't justify – at least, not yet. If you met the target, say so. If you didn't, admit it. That's what they want to know first. Next tell your boss what Actions (A) you have taken since your last meeting: "I have done A and B but not C because ..." Now that you have gained their confidence that you are telling it as it is, you can move to your Proposals (P) – the things you need from your boss to do your job. If your proposals involve spending money, ensure you use the selling steps outline earlier – that is, make sure you link your proposal to the outcomes your boss is seeking. Then, to demonstrate that you are thinking as a senior executive across the organisation and not just about your own departmental issues, offer ideas outside of your area of control – things you notice that might be useful to your boss. Finally, tell your boss some of the decisions you have taken – not because you are asking for permission, but to demonstrate that you are using your delegated power. Bosses love that to know that their lieutenants are extensions of their power. Start your sentence with: "Just to let you know that last month I decided that ..." I tried this approach with a boss of whom I was not a little scared. I learned from the programme that before doing RAPID with my boss, I should try to set the tone of the meeting in Adult-Adult mode by opening the conversation with some small talk. Usually, I would wait for my boss to speak. This time I opened with, "Hi X, how's your knee?" My boss was a runner and had injured his knee. "Much better," he replied. "I may be able to do a half-marathon soon." And so our conversation opened on a light note and then I moved on to the R in RAPID. My proactive approach transformed our meetings. He hadn't changed. I had. These approaches may not always work, but you must take a risk and if you want things to change in your relationships, you must change first.

12. Ask your boss for help – you may get it

I was 30 when I got my first divisional managing director role. I was young and inexperienced. But I was lucky. I had a good group CEO boss from whom I could learn. I learned two unforgettable lessons from him. The first was about the importance of having a chair's backing on a board. I went to him with an issue concerning certain behaviour of members of the senior team which I felt might jeopardise a pending contract renewal. He asked me what I was I going to do about it: "You're the MD, after all!" he said. I said I was hoping he would sort it. He pushed me to say what I would like to do. I said that I would like to raise the matter at the next board meeting under 'any other business' (AOB). He said, "Do that and I'll back you." So, under AOB at the next divisional board meeting which my boss chaired, I said: "Colleagues will be aware that we are up against it in the next contract round and I'm concerned that certain behaviour by some members of the senior team might jeopardise that renewal. Will colleagues join with me in stamping it out?" Members of the board were outraged and rounded on me, asking how I dared besmirch the character of colleagues. The attack on me went on for what seemed like an age and I wondered whether the chair was ever going to intervene, when he said: "You all know Ciarán is telling the truth." There was total silence, followed by a decision to outlaw the behaviour. After the board meeting, one of the directors said to me that that decision was well "overdue". I will never forget the chair's backing.

The other lesson I learned from him was never to bluff. I told him that our main core business suppliers were threatening to increase the price of their services – a significant supply agreement – more than we could afford in the contract renewal budget. He asked me what I was going to do about it, since "you are the MD!" I said I didn't know what to do. I asked his advice. "Go find the same services elsewhere at the price you can afford in your budget. Then tell your opposite number at your supplier that unless they matched that price you are going to leave." "But leaving is a huge task and major disruption," I said. "I know," he replied, "and so do your suppliers. Do it, but don't bluff. If you can't get it elsewhere at the price you want, you have to stay and cut somewhere else. If you can, you have leverage." I did. I found a supplier at the price we could afford – only too glad to have our business. I told our existing supplier that if they didn't match the price, we would leave. He didn't. We left. They lost the contract. I learned about not bluffing. But most of all, I learned that it pays to risk asking your boss for advice – that's what they're paid to do.

Notes

1   Mental Health Foundation, www.mentalhealth.org.uk/explore-mental-health/publications/relationships-21st-century-forgotten-foundation-mental-health-and-well-being.
2   An informal behaviour agreement between two parties.
3   Martin McGuinness and Ian Paisley were sworn enemies during the Troubles in Northern Ireland but became good friends and were nicknamed the 'Chuckle Brothers' during the successful Good Friday/Belfast Agreement negotiations in 1998.
4   10/20/70 rule of change: a variation on the well-established 70:20:10 rule of learning.
5   David Herbert Donald, *Lincoln*, Simon & Schuster, 1995.
6   Doris Kearns Goodwin, *Team of Rivals: The Political Genius of Abraham Lincoln*, Penguin, 2009.
7   *Ibid.*
8   *Ibid.*

Chapter 4: Your key relationships in any organisation – how to view them

1. You

For those of you dipping into the book, let's start by slaying some management-speak tropes, which I discussed in Chapter 1. You are not a human capital asset. No one is. Check your body. Any barcodes? Check your employer client's asset register. Are you on it? No. Is human capital on your employer client's balance sheet? No. Of course not. If they could, accountants would have found a way by now. But they haven't because they can't. Human capital doesn't exist. Never has. Never will. No amount of metaphorical mind-bending will change that fact. No organisation owns you. Of course, you are – technically speaking – a human resource to the extent that you are human, and you are a resource to your organisation. But people see themselves as neither human capital assets nor human resources, and that's what counts. Once, when facilitating a workshop with a group of HRDs, I asked, "Hands up if you love being a human resource." No hands. It's shocking but unsurprising that these HRDs could not find a way to speak their truth in their own system. So don't use the term 'human capital' in relation to yourself or anyone else. It has no place in an ESG-compliant organisation. You are a career micro-business wholly owning your own career equity in the business of your career a function of your CV; your EQ and your reputation (PR) (see Chapter 2). Your job is a joint venture with the other micro-businesses in your organisation for a term. These terms are becoming increasingly brief. That you can count on. Your organisation exists only in law. Otherwise, it's a construct. Some say: "Our people are our greatest asset." No. They're not your assets. They're not even assets.

2. Family and friends

I always knew that family and friends are important, but never more acutely than when I was in and out of hospital in isolation over a year going through chemotherapy and a stem-cell transplant treatment for lymphoma. There, on dark days, I had to confront my purpose. Rather embarrassingly, having asked clients routinely to tell me what their purpose is, I had not confronted my own. My cancer counsellor advised me to read Viktor Frankl's *Man's Search for Meaning*[1] – not because my situation was comparable to his in a concentration camp, but because she knew the book would help me to connect with my intention in life in adversity. It did. I figured out that my purpose, like his, was centred on the people I care about and who care about me. That focus helped him survive and helped me get through some very low moments in isolation for weeks with no visitors due to COVID-19. It's not that I didn't care about people before I had cancer, or that I only care about people who care about me; it's more that people come first for me now where, sometimes, my work came first previously. And I know from my work with in-house lawyers that this is a familiar story. We kid ourselves into thinking that we are working all the hours for our loved ones because we have no option but to play the game, because we can't fix the system which demands so much of our time. And we feel that we must provide a standard of living commensurate with assumptions as to what is expected of us. But we have more options than we admit to ourselves. I had an option to downsize much earlier than I did. I could have sold our house and moved to a less expensive area, reducing financial and health risks and – crucially – creating more discretionary time for those I care about and who care about me. I didn't. It was a big mistake in my career. I and my family suffered because of my stress, and because of the insecurity of the famine/feast rollercoaster of one-man-band consulting. I didn't assess the risks. I assumed I had no choice but to deliver a certain standard of living and that at some point things would work out. They didn't. The rollercoaster meant that unbearable stress and debt followed my unconscious risk-taking as sure as day followed night. Lockdown was the tipping point. My revenues collapsed. We had to downsize our lifestyles significantly. I used to feel unbearable shame about this – so much so that I was in denial about the unconscious risks I took in my business. But having worked on how shame has blighted my life, I can now write and talk about it, not in shame, but in truth. I can forgive myself and those I care about have forgiven me. For the balance of my career, I will never, ever take unconscious risks again. So, my appeal to you as an in-house lawyer is to prioritise your loved ones above every other relationship except your relationship with yourself, which must come first. If you are stressed, listen to your body. Don't ignore it. If your identity is so connected with your in-house career that you find you are prioritising your work above your family and friends, this is a red light. Richard Martin, a faculty colleague of mine on Paul Gilbert's LBCambridge2 programme for senior in-house lawyers,[2] spent 20 years as an employment lawyer before a significant mental breakdown led to his hospitalisation and a two-year recovery period out of work. In 2018 he published his memoir – *This Too Will Pass: Anxiety in a Professional World*[3] – in which he describes his breakdown and recovery and how he didn't see it coming. Read it and avoid the error that he, and I, made. See it coming.

3. Society, the profession and the regulators

When I ask in-house lawyers about their most important relationship after their relationship with themselves and their family, they say it's their client. They mean their bosses. I struggle to convince them that their most important relationship should be society – the S in ESG – represented by the court and the rule of law. In-house lawyers play a key role in their organisations, bringing much to their work, including beyond their core legal experience. But their primary role is to practise law. They are bound by specific regulatory and professional obligations, which include a duty to act with independence and to give precedence to their professional obligations over the interests of their client employer. Recent corporate scandals have put in-house regulation and practice in the spotlight, highlighting the tension between in-house lawyers' requirement of independence and their status as an employee. My proposition to you as an in-house lawyer is to reconnect with your relationship with society, the court, your profession, and to reframe your expectations of your regulators. Of the latter, I encourage you to demand their support of your independence and I cover this matter later in this book. I also encourage you to refer to your in-house career as the *practice* of law in-house – not a word I hear used often by your colleagues; and to speak openly about upholding the promise you made to society when you received your practising certificate. Act as if society comes first, and it will. I suspect that you and many readers will baulk – if not laugh – at this invitation. You and they will see it as naïve. But for reasons which will become clear later in the book, I believe that this reframing of your in-house mindset as the practice of law in-house in the service of society, of which your employer client is a member, will improve your relationships, your health, your wellbeing; and you will serve your employer client and society better accordingly.

4. Your employer client

'Employer client' is not, I suspect a term, you use. The terms my in-house lawyer clients use include: 'the business', 'my line manager', 'my boss' and 'my CEO'. But they are not your client. You know this is true because you are a lawyer. You know that your relationship with your employer client is with a corporate body, not with a person – not with your boss, your CEO or your chief financial officer (CFO), however unreal that feels in a dysfunctional system. I appreciate that it must feel unreal to you, given that those individuals control your pay, promotion and annual review. So, my advice to you is to live the truth of your legal relationship with your employer client. Use the term. You will feel awkward using that term initially. But you and they will get used to it.

By living that truth, you will create environments for yourself and others in which you all can thrive. Any other basis for the relationship is living a lie. But how can you live that relationship realistically? The answer is to behave in your relationships to reflect that reality. 'Act as if ...' is a well-established behaviour change model – for example, as set out in the best-selling book *Feel the Fear and Do It Anyway*,[4] in which you are advised to act as if you are not afraid and, over time, you may well learn not to be afraid. It's about courage. From the vantage point of acting as if the truth of your legal relationship with your employer client were the reality, you can engage primarily with your organisation's purpose – why it does what it does – rather than primarily with your bosses. You can reframe the politics of your relationship in an instant. All it takes is for you to decide to do it. Now. Your purpose as a lawyer and your employer client's purpose are interdependent. Your employer client's purpose must, as the emphasis on ESG grows in importance, involve the needs of society, to which you owe an overarching duty. So, I'm proposing a reframing of your relationship based on that interdependence of purposes. Your purpose as a lawyer is to enable better decisions and processes in the service of the purpose of your employer client – which, society demands, is ultimately about creating a sustainable organisation that honours all, not just some, stakeholders. This involves a mindset change. Think of yourself as a corporate doctor focused on the long-term health of the corporate body. I'm not suggesting that this mindset is easy if, for example, the personality of your boss or others in the organisation makes you feel that corporate purpose is synonymous with their purpose. In later chapters, I explain how to mitigate that behaviour.

4.1 The purpose of your employer client

Your relationship with your employer client's purpose is the foundation stone of that relationship. Are you comfortable with it? In recent years, the word 'purpose' has become popular because the fundamentals of capitalism are under scrutiny by society, which is challenging the traditional purpose of business. But its ubiquity has led to some dilution in its meaning. The word 'purpose' is a noun meaning why you do something or why something exists. It's not a proper noun – that is, it is not written with a capital letter. So, your organisation can use the

Your relationship with your employer client's strategy will define how you practise law in your organisation. Your organisation's strategy is a statement of how it intends to achieve its purpose. It's no less than that. But no more. Are you comfortable with it?

word as it likes: "Our purpose is to maximise returns to shareholders"; or "Our purpose is to be the best no-frills airline in the world"; or "Our purpose is to make widgets profitably and to benefit society." The problem with all trends in business is that language is the first casualty. Management-speak is designed to distance us from truths. So instead of taking the time to say, "Our purpose goes beyond making money – we also care about the impact we are having on society," the current trend demands that we use the term 'purpose-led' or 'purpose-driven' as if the word 'purpose' has one meaning – the meaning assumed by the user. This is not a matter of semantics and I'm not suggesting that people who use the term 'purpose-led' are wrong. In fact, I share their intention and those deeply involved in the purpose movement are delivering a great service to society and to business. My point is that in-house lawyers need to be guardians of language because words are key to their profession. We rely on them to use words with precision. So, to manage your relationship with your employer client, you need to contribute to the framing of its purpose to ensure that it embraces a purpose that includes society. You can also contribute to ensuring that the purpose statement is shared by all at the top of the organisation. If it's not, then it's difficult to deliver on a purpose that is not shared.

4.2 Your employer client's strategy

Your relationship with your employer client's strategy will define how you practise law in your organisation. Your organisation's strategy is a statement of how it intends to achieve its purpose. It's no less than that. But no more. Are you comfortable with it? Despite its overuse in management-speak, 'strategy' means only 'how' an organisation achieves its 'why'. That's it. Never in the history of business has one word suffered as much abuse. The most overused form of the word is 'strategic' – especially when it is linked with the breathtakingly woolly word 'stuff', as in: "My team does the day-to-day stuff"; or "I concentrate on the strategic stuff"; or "I'm appointing a COO so that I can concentrate on the strategic stuff." The imprecise language is the clue to a lack of understanding of what the word 'strategy' means.

The reason that there's so much management-speak about strategy is because it's hard work to get right. It's difficult because it must be simple to succeed. And simple strategies are awesomely difficult to conceive and implement. One of the best examples of a simple strategy was the start-up strategy of European no-frills airline Ryanair: to irritate as many customers as possible, so that all they expected was a cheap and safe flight. This strategy looks obvious with hindsight. But there was a time when British Airways was – as its ads proudly and with some justification declared – the world's greatest airline. Only affluent people then flew in planes. They expected five-star treatment and paid five-star prices. Michael O'Leary – and others – decided that air travel could be democratised. And with the help of enabling technology – the Internet – they did. British Airways almost collapsed.

When I work with main and executive boards and teams, I am frequently shocked by directors using the word 'strategy' instead of 'plan', as in: "We've done loads of work on our strategy and produced a 30-slide deck." I say to them that they must be able to summarise their shared – and it must be shared – strategy in one or two lines; and that their 30-slide deck may be their plan, but it's not their strategy. It's impossible to have a shared strategy without a shared purpose. Many boards lack a shared purpose. In 1996, Michael Porter – regarded as a leading strategy thinker – wrote a long article: "What Is Strategy?"[5] You should read it. It should be prescribed reading for all main and executive board members, even if they read only his key three principles – that strategy "is the creation of a unique and valuable position ... serving [needs] ... requires you to make trade-offs in competing – to choose what not to do ... [and] involves creating 'fit' among a company's activities".[6]

You can encourage high-quality conversations about strategy among your employer client's main and executive board and teams. First, you need to understand the word. Then you need not be afraid to stick your oar in on strategy. Don't bemoan the fact – as many of your colleagues do – that in-house lawyers are not invited to the 'top table' – a frequently used term at in-house lawyer conferences and in articles. Demonstrate, rather than assert, your understanding of business purpose and strategy and the contribution that your practice of law in-house can make to shaping your employer client's purpose and strategy at a time of greater emphasis on ESG – a topic which is increasingly at the heart of your legal practice in-house.

4.3 Your employer client's behaviour plan

Your relationship with your organisation's behaviour plan – operating plan or target operating model – will help you to decide what it needs in terms of legal counsel and process. Your organisation's behaviour plan consists of those actions it takes and avoids, consciously or unconsciously, to implement its strategy to achieve its purpose. Conscious actions include the implementation of business plans including sales and marketing plans and target operating models. Target operating models identify market needs, resources and processes to implement those resources to meet the market needs. Unconscious and avoidance behaviour includes all those actions which are not taken in respect of the implementation of your organisation's strategy.

4.4 Your employer client's main board

Your relationship with your main board – whether close or not – is key because it represents your client. As you know, society through its laws grants your client employer a mandate to trade as a separate legal entity – a veil which protects your employers. The nature of that mandate granted by society to organisations is undergoing rapid change. That veil is being lifted more frequently. Society is concerned about the conduct of boards – their behaviour over time – in respect of the impact of their decisions on ESG. It is no longer a one-way street. Your role in the governance of your employer client's decision-making processes on its main board, no matter what level you are at in the organisation, is key.

4.5 Your employer client's chair

Your attitude to the chair of your organisation – again, whether close or not, whether you meet them or not – is key. They ultimately are the most important representative of your client employer organisation. View them as your ultimate boss whether they are good chairs or not. If they're not good, you should consider moving elsewhere or explore whether you can take steps with colleagues to mitigate the risks of a poor chair. If they are good at their job, try to meet them if you don't regularly; and if you do, learn from them. Their role is unique in organisations because they perform three functions that no one else can or should do: to decide when the board should sack its CEO; to take ultimate responsibility for governance of the organisation; and to ensure that the board is effective in its decision making.

A strong chair will know when to raise the sacking of the CEO with the board. It's difficult for others to do so. A weak chair, on the other hand, makes the CEO in that case the *de facto* executive chair. That combination is not good for the organisation or anyone in it. Weak chairs abound because the entire non-executive world is systemically weak. If it were strong, there would be fewer corporate scandals and, arguably, we would not have had a Global Financial Crash in 2008 – or at least its scale would have been considerably less. The chair is responsible for governance and, in the United Kingdom, the Financial Reporting Council (FRC) Corporate Governance Code 2018[7] and the accompanying guidance is as good a guide as any for chairs, even if your organisation is not required to comply with its provisions. These are excellent and useful documents. The only problem with the FRC code that it must assume strong chairs will apply it. And they don't.

'Board effectiveness' is an irritating use of language because it panders to management-speak by converting an adjective to a noun. Management-speak uses distancing nouns like 'effectiveness' and 'engagement' instead of adjectives like 'effective' and 'engaging' because the latter require us to take more responsibility for their veracity. Your chair is responsible for ensuring that your board is effective. The most effective boards are those where the chair creates an environment in which members feel they can always call out behaviour they feel is inappropriate or address any issue. An effective board is marked by one where fear is absent.

4.6 Your employer client's NEDs
Your employer client's NEDs are the NEDs on your main board. 'Non-executive' means that they should not be involved in the day-to-day running of the business which is carried out by your executive board. I

say 'should not' because some NEDs attempt to be both CEO and chair; and they shouldn't. Equally, some NEDs behave as if they have only influence and no power. The law is clear on this point: it draws no distinction between executive directors and NEDs in terms of duties. You can Google the roles and responsibilities of NEDs. You will find that there are courses galore (including my own) on how they should act and behave; but it all boils down to one requirement which you will not see in any legislation or guidance: the executive directors should respect their NEDs. Respect is noble. We feel it when we approach speed cameras, the police and our boss if they are good leaders. The FRC guidance is particularly helpful in fleshing out key issues. But the code does not or cannot address the individual behaviour change needs of each NED, as these are unique individuals. The most common behaviour change need I encounter with NEDs is to own their power as directors, fully. Had all the NEDs on the boards of the key banks before 2007 – and those on the boards of companies hit by major corporate scandals before and after the Global Financial Crash in 2008 – used their power, much pain, suffering and economic damage would have been avoided, most of which was experienced by those genuinely with no power or voice in those boardrooms.

I find that new NEDs are particularly prone to imposter syndrome – even, and sometimes especially, those who would have been regarded as tough CEOs or directors in their corporate careers. Their lack of confidence stems more often from an unaccustomed feeling that they don't or can't control the board. They are used to wielding power. Now they feel they have none. They play a zero-sum game: "If I can't run this, then who am I?" But there is a mid-point between feeling the need to have total power and none, and that is: influencing from a position of power. In 2016, I covered some of these issues in a pamphlet, *The Seven Deadly Sins of Nascent NEDs*.[8]

5. Your boss

Your boss is likely to be your CEO, your CFO or another lawyer. Whoever it is, their job in relation to you is to create an environment in which you thrive. That many bosses do not take this duty seriously does not

Your boss is likely to be your CEO, your CFO or another lawyer. Whoever it is, their job in relation to you is to create an environment in which you thrive.

negate their obligation to you to do so – or indeed your own obligation those you lead. In your head, you should expect them to take care of you. If you feel that statement is laughable or unrealistic, you are missing the point of this book. This book is about how you can improve your relationships at work by adopting the highest standards of behaviour at work, irrespective of the degree to which others – including your bosses – fall short of those standards. What difference, you may reasonably ask, will these aspirational high standards make to your boss if they don't care about creating an environment in which you and others thrive? The answer is that you will have figured out well in advance what your boundaries are and, if crossed by your boss, you will be prepared to take appropriate action even if that action means it's time for you to find a different environment in which you have a better chance of thriving. Moreover, you will radiate a clarity of personal PSB which your boss will sense if not know and may in time come to respect. Your -ism (see Chapter 2) will be clear to them. In my case, that's Ciarán-ism. People who know me know my -ism. Some like my -ism, some don't. But they know it; and they know when mine changes because you are allowed to change your -ism. What's your -ism? I explore this in more detail in other chapters. Meanwhile, please bear in mind that if you were trained in private practice, I suspect that your expectations of the standards of leadership behaviour of your bosses was low, and that you were surprised if some were high. The criticisms which law firms receive in annual wellbeing reports are reasonable grounds for this suspicion.

If you are the most senior lawyer in your organisation – usually titled GC or head of legal – your line manager is likely to be your CEO or your CFO. Although these reporting lines are the norm, I encourage you to believe – for reasons set out in more detail later – that they are damaging to your relationships, to your career, to your organisation and to society. You are conflicted. You should report to the chair or to the senior independent director on your board, not to another lawyer. Those reporting lines would maximise your ability to act with independence. If you report to the CFO or to the COO, I encourage you to find a way, urgently, to change your reporting line at least to the CEO. From what I have witnessed, these second-tier reporting lines create additional risks to your ability to act with independence, with consequent impact on risks to the organisation and to society. If you report to a lawyer who is a GC or a deputy GC or head of legal, you should be aware of the risks in their reporting lines because these affect your relationships. If your boss is a lawyer, bear in mind that they have a responsibility to create an environment in which you thrive. You will either disagree with my view above or, if you agree with it, you will wonder what the point is in bearing in the mind the widespread dysfunctionality of the current system of reporting lines. If the former, I hope you change your mind by the time you finish reading this book. If the latter, then the reason you should wake up every day conscious of the systemic weakness in the current practice of law in-house is that you will not practise law unconsciously. Unconscious behaviour is the enemy of productive, safe and rewarding relationships. You may even – as others are doing – find the courage to speak up in your organisation about the dangers to it of your reporting line.

6. The executive board

The day-to-day relationships of most in-house lawyers are with the senior leadership team or their direct reports – sometimes referred to as the executive committee, operating board or executive board. It's important to understand the purpose of each role on the executive board so that in managing your relationship with them, you can understand their perspective, concerns and stress levels. You may find, for example, *The Changing C-Suite*[9] by José Luis Alvarez and Silviya Svejenova – in which they examine "the evolving ways in which power at the apex of complex organisations is structured through roles and relationships" – a useful stimulation for reflection on the "emergence and evolution of these CXO roles". The following notes are mine.

6.1 The CEO
The CEO of your employer client should – like all leaders – create an environment in which the people they lead thrive, grow your organisation and serve all its stakeholders. They should inspire all but lead only a few – the people on their executive board. They need to understand what each person on their board needs to thrive and to help

them meet those needs. This is tough work. It's emotionally demanding. It's their job to help the people they lead be the best they can be. It's also the CEO's job to ensure that the people at the top of the organisation agree on a shared PSB, to implement the strategy to grow the organisation. The keyword is 'shared'. Many CEOs don't lead the painful process of facilitating a shared purpose. Consequently, their strategy is misdirected and their plans go awry. CEO's must maximise profit but not at the cost of ESG.

The change you can help the executive board embrace is that the ESG movement is not going to diminish or disband. It's not a fad. It has its problems and is guilty of greenwashing, for sure, but it will endure because it speaks to a universal truth that everyone understands: we must protect our environment or we will perish; we must serve society or, sooner or later, it will rise in rebellion and outrage as history demonstrates – universal suffrage, equality before the law, #MeToo and Black Lives Matter to mention a few movements which ensured their voices were heard and that their messages would endure. Your executive board, led by your CEO, can't protect our environment or serve society unless it governs – takes decisions – which take the environment and society into account. Your role in creating an environment of good governance is key. You can discharge this duty best by consistently championing good decision-making processes. You must know what these are and how the CEO should be modelling them. If you report to the CEO in your organisation, try to secure a dotted reporting line to the chair or senior independent director to bolster your independence.

6.2 The CFO

Your CFO outranks everyone else when it comes to the numbers. Every number. They have a key strategic role: they must confirm, or not, whether the agreed strategy stacks financially. No one else can or should make that call. They are responsible for signing off budgets and accounts, and they control cash. I have a soft spot for CFOs. I was cajoled into a cost and management accounting traineeship after university and hated every minute of it, initially. Begrudgingly, I made peace with it and by the age of 29 – by which stage I was a financial controller, before moving into my first divisional managing director role I had become a reasonably good accountant. I will never forget the evenings, all-nighters and weekends in my 20s spent doing budgets, reconciling accounts and preparing the monthly pack for the board: the balance sheet, the profit and loss account and notes on the variances against budget. I will also never forget doing my first bank reconciliation, the first of hundreds and what happened when I presented it proudly to my boss. "Does it balance?" he asked. "Yes," I replied. "No, it doesn't," he said. "Well, it's only a few thousand pounds out," I said. "Well, a few thousand pounds out could be the net of umpteen large debit or credit entry errors either way," he said. "Do it again – to the penny!" he insisted. I did. He was right. There were lots of posting errors – some huge. And they did net out to a few thousand pounds. An appreciation of the power, beauty and elegance of the double-entry accounting system has never left me since. My training and experiences as an accountant in those early years still come in useful in my work with leaders and boards. CFOs know that there are no shortcuts in accounting.

CFOs are usually inexperienced in other functions – especially sales, marketing and information technology. They sometimes fail to listen to people who do know what they are talking about, leading to painful reforecasting at best and serious business injury at worst. The CFO and the legal function are frequently at loggerheads because the CFO is under pressure to maximise profit and the legal function must sometimes challenge their conduct in doing so in the service of creating a sustainable organisation. Some CFOs who become CEOs don't understand that they can't cherry-pick the aspects of the CEO role that they like best. Some struggle and retreat into their beloved spreadsheets and don't allow their successor CFOs to do their jobs, resulting in a weak CEO and a weak CFO – a dangerous combination.

6.3 The COO

The role and purpose of your COO are to keep your organisation's promise with your customers. Nothing else, in my view. Some boards like to say that their COO runs the business day to day, and their CEO runs strategy. I don't agree with this view. Your CEO must run the business day to day. But only your COO is responsible for customer satisfaction. In the old days, they were called 'heads of production' or 'head of services'. Today they are 'heads of delivery'. 'Delivery' is the one management-speak word I have tried to stop using but can't. I wrote to Lucy Kellaway when she was the doyenne of eliminating management-speak at the *Financial Times* to ask her advice on the use of the word. "Never," she replied, "should the word 'delivery' appear in a sentence in which a white van does not also appear." We have all failed this test. The word 'delivery' is ubiquitous in business. Your role in supporting delivery is key – not least because of the centrality of legal contracts in delivery of good and services.

6.4 The chief revenue officer/sales director

Your chief revenue officer (CRO) or sales director is responsible for generating revenue and, in management-speak, they own the revenue number in the accounts. In this context, the word 'own' means they are blamed – often shamed – when the monthly variance between actual and budgeted sales is negative and celebrated – often overly so – when the variance is positive. I experienced this rollercoaster feeling most acutely in one financial year when I owned the sales number as a divisional director of a large organisation. I was on the executive committee which met weekly and usually, the management accounts for the previous month were presented at the first executive committee meeting of the month. Any director who owned a sales number would be feeling nervous at that meeting if there were brackets around their names (negative variances against budget had brackets around them). In January of that year, I was celebrated warmly by the CEO because my sales variance was healthily positive and, since I was responsible for turning around an underperforming division, he saw the variance as a positive omen for the full year. I didn't. The positive variance filled me with dread. I knew that he had forgotten that the phasing of the revenue budget – that is, how the projected revenues were spread across the year – were kind, to put it mildly, to our division in January. So, he brought champagne to our floor to celebrate our results and praised me to the high heavens at the executive board meeting. I dreaded February's results, with good reason. The phasing for February was much tougher and we missed – I missed – the monthly target significantly. I knew that I would. I had protested to the finance director during the budget round that the full year's revenue budget was not achievable unless the marketing spend was significantly increased. He refused, so I was stuck with a revenue number I knew I couldn't achieve. This conduct is common. So, at the March executive committee meeting, at which the February results were presented, the CEO turned and looked at me balefully and used the shaming word most dreaded by executive board members: 'disappointed'. "Ciarán's results are disappointing, to say the least," he said slowly. You could smell the *schadenfreude* in the room as those not in the firing line savoured the discomfort of another. My variances became worse each month until around mid-year, relief came in the form of every CRO's favourite words: the revenue reforecast – the revised year-end budget phased over the remaining months of the year. A new column was inserted into the management accounts, headed "Reforecast"; and while the variance against budget was still reported, the variance that mattered politically at executive board meetings was the variance against the reforecast. The trick, of course, is to justify to the CFO the most conservative reforecast possible and with the most realistic phasing. For example, if August is a quiet month, then the revenue reforecast for August should be as low as possible without putting too much pressure on the other months. I managed to achieve a realistic reforecast and my life for the rest of the year was less miserable.

So, in-house lawyers will benefit in their relationships with the sales function if they demonstrate to the salespeople that they understand the political and budget dynamics under which they work. Help them if you can – as one GC did when he spotted a helpful and legitimate change in accounting treatment for sales. But make clear to them at the beginning of the year that when you say no, you mean no on legal issues relating to sales – not because you are a deal blocker, but because you too must do your job as a regulated professional. If you clearly contract your relationship with the revenue function at the start, you can say they were warned. You can't do this if you don't understand the detail of the pressure under which the sales function operates.

6.5 The chief marketing officer

Lawyers generally tend not to understand marketing, in my experience. Attitudes to marketing vary considerably between sectors. The best marketers I've worked with are in the food and drink sector. The good ones are very clever. It's a complex and stressful job. One chief marketing officer (CMO) I worked with relaunched a high-profile confectionery brand which he said had lost its way. I love that phrase and hear it often. It makes me want to call a sort of marketing coastguard. To turn the brand around, he took risks with campaign decisions which had to be taken months ahead of production decisions. Get those wrong and your confection is toast, as it were. He got it right and the brand – a household name – recovered. On the other hand, the worst marketing behaviour I witness is in professional services. I repeat this anecdote through the book: "What's all this fuss about marketing?" fumed one multimillion-dollar equity partner client to me. "The only marketing we need in this business is 40 tickets to Wimbledon." The art and science of marketing were trashed by him in one sentence. Kotler[10] said that marketing is about the four Ps: product, price, place and promotion. Your CMO must get all these right or the sales director won't make their targets. The best favour in-house lawyers could do to the marketing function is to demonstrate that they understand marketing principles. Kotler is a good place to start.

6.6 The chief technology officer

Many people at the top of organisations don't know what they don't know about how technology can enable business strategy. I learned this truth through an embarrassing lesson when in 1995 I was appointed managing director of a division of a large business. I was young, inexperienced and excited. It was a great role with global growth opportunities. On my first day, I had a meeting with the group chief technology officer (CTO). I told him what I wanted in technology terms to assist my strategy for world domination. He looked at me witheringly and said, "Ciarán, congratulations on your appointment and I wish you well as managing director, but I am the group CTO and in future, please can you bring me a problem and not a solution?" I blushed. I'll never forget that lesson and often tell the story to clients on boards who struggle to respect, value and understand other function leaders.

The other story I tell them is of the CTO I witnessed say "No" to their CEO on an executive board. The CEO was adamant that the organisation would have to achieve a major technology transformation by a certain date for good business reasons, but also because it would constitute a major PR coup. The CTO said that it wouldn't be ready by that date. The CEO was no shrinking violet and most of the executive board were afraid to challenge him. But the CTO did. I'll never forget it. It's surprising to me the number of start-ups, growth businesses and even mature professional services businesses that do not have a CTO on their operating boards. That's self-harm in corporate terms. It just doesn't make sense not to have a technology voice at the table. Lawyers have a chequered historical relationship with technology but the key to having a good relationship with the IT function is to ask questions. They like to be asked questions because it demonstrates respect for their knowledge. Plenty of open biased questions. 'Open' as in: who? What? When? Where? Why? 'Biased' in the sense that the bias of your questions should be towards an understanding of the relationship between technology and strategy.

6.7 The HRD

Your HRD has a difficult role. Frequently the Cinderella of the executive board, they are often lampooned, ignored and under-resourced. Yet they are the victim of the failure of CEOs all over the world to acknowledge that they, not the HR function, are responsible for creating an environment in which people in their organisation thrive. The role of HR is to support the CEO in creating that environment and to manage what has become known as transactional human resources activity and systems – all the activity not related to training, culture and behaviour. As discussed earlier, and I repeat the point here for those dipping into the book: HRDs are also the victim of the myth of human capital. It doesn't exist. If it did, the accountants would have found a way by now of putting people on the balance sheet. They haven't. Human resources do exist in the sense that people are human and are resources to the organisation. But no one sees themselves as human resources – not even HRDs. I know this because I asked a group of them at a workshop to put up their hands if they loved being a human capital asset/human resource. No hands went up. No surprise. It's all tosh. Proof, if proof were needed, is the number of HR conferences that still debate the role and purpose of HR. Only in-house lawyers match HR in this annual futility. You will not see CFOs, CTOs, COOs, CMOs or CROs debate their roles at conferences. They may debate their evolving role but not their purpose. Their purpose is clear to them. I encourage you, therefore, to avoid the terms 'human capital' and 'human resources'. They undermine the dignity of the people who work in your organisation. In *Leading with Dignity*, Donna Hicks concludes that: "dignity not only explains an aspect of what it means to be human, but also a hallmark of our shared humanity ... Everyone wants to be treated in a way that shows they matter."[11]

You want to matter too. So, practise law in house with dignity and with the dignity of others in mind; and when you can, use the words 'people' or 'employees'. The dignity of employees would be better served if the title HRD were replaced by the title 'chief of staff', which is gaining in popularity, and whose role would be to help leaders create an environment in which the people they lead can be what they can be and therefore can thrive. All legal and accounting matters relating to people could be manged by the legal function and by the finance function. You, as an in-house lawyer with some responsibility for good governance in your organisation, might consider gently promoting the value of the chief of staff model to better individual and organisational outcomes.

7. External advisers and providers

The key external relationship of the legal function is with out-of-house counsel. Other external providers include specialists, such as legal technology providers and those working in what has become known as 'new law'. It's a mark of the glacial pace of change in the profession that, many years on, it's still known as 'new law'. I want to focus here on your relationship with outside counsel and the firms for which they work. One of the most political and complex relationships is the relationship between law functions and law firms. For many in-house lawyers, their favourite out-of-house lawyers are almost part of the team. In many cases, those lawyers come from the law firms in which they were trained. Frequently, outside counsel are sought for air cover on occasions in which the in-house lawyer is perfectly capable of making a legal judgement call. This practice drives up legal costs and dilutes the power of the in-house lawyer. In addition, usually GCs are reluctant to allow law firms access to their management teams, fearing loss of control. One law firm partner told me that a GC had severely rebuked him for chatting to a board member and had suggested that if that reoccurred, the firm would not be instructed again. The partner decided to close the relationship, saying they wanted to receive no further instructions. No winners there. On the other hand, law firms are often content – perhaps unconsciously – to take advantage of the weakness in the relationship between the legal function and their employer clients. A weak GC can mean more fees for the law firm. The in-house/out-of-house/employer client relationship is dysfunctional, in my view, and I deal with fixing the relationship elsewhere in the book. There appears to be no appetite to change the situation systemically. However, you don't have to wait for systemic change to reframe your attitude to external lawyers. Start by confronting the truths contained in the language you use, and everyone uses to describe them and you. Why are you and your colleagues called in-house lawyers while your colleague accountants are not called in-house accountants? Nor are your IT colleagues. Why not? What is the difference between you and your accountant or IT colleagues? The difference, as you know, is that you are a regulated lawyer with a duty to act with independence as well as an overriding duty to protect society and uphold the rule of law as an officer of the court. Your colleague accountant is not in that precise position, although they do, for sure, have obligations to their regulators. The term 'in-house lawyer' does imply therefore, does it not, that you are a regulated lawyer practising in-house, not out-of-house? The problem for you is that your colleague accountant is an employee with a relatively uncomplicated relationship with their employer; whereas your employer is also your client, in respect of which you must act with independence. The complexities and potential conflict in this relationship are obvious. Yet your profession, your regulators and your employers have ducked this problem for many years. As I write, and as set out elsewhere in this book, there are signs that some of your colleague in-house lawyers are calling time on this dangerous impasse. My advice to you is to join them. Meanwhile, your out-of-house counsel could be enlisted in your task of reframing your in-house legal function's relationship with your employer client. They could – perhaps should – invest time and resources for free to gain a deeper understanding of the issues in your organisation. This would require new behaviour by some GCs in including their out-of-house colleagues in meetings with their employer clients to create a shared understanding of the link between business purpose and strategy and the legal counsel, and the process required to implement that strategy to achieve that purpose. Of course, this would require law firms to change their current behaviour and invest deeply in their relationships. Until now, there has been little incentive for them to do so. But they know that the in-house community is starting to voice its concerns about how it is supported by regulators (see Chapter 6) to prevent harm to them and to society. It won't be long before these shifts lead to a reframing of the relationship between GCs and law firms, leading to an incentive for them to change their behaviour. Already some GCs tell me that they will not instruct law firm ESG practices if the law firm is not demonstrating that it practises what it preaches in its care for ESG. That said, with the billable hour and partnership model still firmly in place, it will take a quantum shift in GC client behaviour to change the behaviour of law firms. I suspect that this shift will come soon and when it comes, it will come suddenly – big bang fashion. Wise law firm managing partners will be preparing for this outcome.

8. Your legal team

Your relationships with your in-house lawyer colleagues, if you have any, need careful management. Relationships within legal teams are frequently fraught. I have found these are sometimes more problematic than the relationship with the employer client. Apart from the usual conflicts that occur in any team, in-house legal teams present unique relationship management challenges. First, by dint of their training as self-reliant individual practitioners, lawyers are not always easily led or always good at leading, are not always necessarily good team players, and can put a strong and sometimes unhelpful emphasis on being the

Seek out, if you can, inspirational lawyer leaders and either work for them or ask them to help you with your career. They will be easy to spot. They will talk about feelings and needs.

brightest person on the room. On one occasion working with in-house teams, I was taken aback at how reluctant some lawyers can be in supporting their GC or head of legal. They were rude and grumpy. Equally, I have witnessed some appallingly poor leadership by GCs whose ascent to the top owed more to sharp elbows than inspirational leadership skills. Second, they often don't know what they don't know about business, sometimes wing it more often than they are willing to admit and are reluctant to embrace change. On more than one occasion I found, in helping to reframe the relationship between the legal function and the board CEO, that the board were amenable to change but some of the lawyers were not so keen on trying out a new model. Third, room for promotion within in-house teams is limited. This can create significant career frustrations, leading to conflict between team members. Good leaders can languish near the top for many years with no sign of their leader willing or being asked to budge or create a sustainable succession plan. That said, I have met truly inspirational GCs, assistant GCs and heads of legal. I also have encountered great mutually supportive teams. My advice to you is to seek out, if you can, inspirational lawyer leaders and either work for them or ask them to help you with your career. They will be easy to spot. They will talk about feelings and needs. Be humble about your business knowledge. Read the top 10 successful business books and ask lots of questions.

Notes

1   Viktor Frankl, *Man's Search for Meaning*, Beacon Press, 1946.
2   www.lbcwisecounsel.com/events-and-workshops/lbcambridge2/speakers/richard-martin/.
3   Richard Martin, *This Too Will Pass: Anxiety in a Professional World*, Trigger, 2018.
4   Susan Jeffers, *Feel The Fear And Do It Anyway*, Vermilion, 2007.
5   Michael Porter, "What Is Strategy?", *Harvard Business Review*, November-December 1996.
6   *Ibid.*
7   Financial Reporting Council (FRC) Corporate Governance Code 2018, www.frc.org.uk/getattachment/88bd8c45-50ea-4841-95b0-d2f4f48069a2/2018-uk-corporate-governance-code-final.pdf.
8   Ciarán Fenton, *The Seven Deadly Sins of Nascent NEDs*, Oaktree Press 2016.
9   José Luis Alvarez and Silviya Svejenova, *The Changing C-Suite*, Oxford University Press, 2021.
10 Philip Kotler, *Marketing Insights from A to Z: 80 Concepts Every Manager Needs to Know*, John Wiley & Sons, 2003.
11 Donna Hicks, *Leading with Dignity: How to Create a Culture That Brings Out the Best in People*, Yale University Press, 2018.

Chapter 5: How to lead teams and work with boards

1. Introduction

This chapter is about how to lead teams and work with boards from your perspective as an in-house lawyer, irrespective of your age or stage in your career. Your legal training in law school, private practice or the bar will have shaped your perspective on leadership, teamwork and how best to work with boards. Most, if not all, of the in-house lawyers with whom I have worked did not study leadership, leading teams or working with employer client boards during their legal training. Their training did not value leadership as a skill. It is not billable by the hour. Furthermore, the skills that are valued in the practice of law and therefore emphasised during legal training eschew the EQ components required in good leadership: empathy, self-awareness and the ability to meet one's needs productively. I have not met one in-house lawyer who reported an emphasis on those three essential components in leadership as skills encouraged in their training and indeed in their practice of law. Even the senior GCs I know who display these leadership qualities naturally are not always fully aware that their

Good leadership for in-house lawyers is about creating an environment in which the people they lead can thrive, growing and developing their legal function and meeting the needs of their stakeholders.

training, the accepted practice of law and the culture of their profession have together muted in them to some extent these natural qualities. My purpose, therefore, in this chapter is to complement the existing excellent canon of general leadership books and articles, the books and material on leading legal teams written by lawyers and the books and articles on boards written by board advisers by focusing on the steps that in-house lawyers can take to connect or reconnect with those skills and qualities essential to leading teams and working with boards which were ignored or discouraged during their legal training. Good leadership for in-house lawyers is about creating an environment in which the people they lead can thrive, growing and developing their legal function and meeting the needs of their stakeholders – including shareholders, employees, customers, suppliers, the court, the environment and society – through excellent governance. The key aspect of working with boards which I explore in this chapter is understanding their nature and dynamics in decision-making behaviour, the cornerstone of governance – a topic of direct interest to you. In relation to how best to work with teams and boards, I explore team and board dynamics themes based on my experiences in board practice.

2. Creating an environment in which people thrive

If you lead or wish to lead a legal team of lawyers and support staff who are not lawyers, your key objective as a leader must be to create an environment in which each member of the team can thrive as an individual and consequently do their best work. This tenet of leadership is well established in leadership research in business and in sport. Not that the approach does not have its detractors. It does. Some favour the stick rather than the carrot. Many GCs and private practice law partners I know do too. If you do, this chapter won't be to your liking because in it, I champion an approach of seeking the Holy Grail of leadership: discretionary effort – that is, effort which the people you lead deliver to you because they believe in your leadership, and not because they are afraid of you or because they are paid to do so. For example, a client who had trained as an officer in the British Army told me that initially during his training, the troops who reported to him addressed him as 'sir', but that one day they started calling him 'boss'. "Why are you calling me 'boss' today?" he asked them. "We have decided that we are ready to trust our lives to you now," they answered. An extreme example, for sure; but one that demonstrates what it takes to get the people you lead to go the extra mile.

You can secure discretionary effort from the people you lead by understanding what motivates them. Some need constant feedback or approval; others need autonomy or a combination of these or other needs. You, or their line managers who report to you, must spend time with them getting to understand their needs. This is time worth investing. The process of understanding their needs is simple: ask them open biased questions. By 'open', I mean questions to which the answer is not yes or no – these are closed questions. By 'biased', I mean questions biased towards finding out what makes them happy at work. However, while the process I recommend is simple, the implementation of that process is not simple, especially with lawyers. They have a notoriously high pain threshold at work. They are often very good at what they do in terms of practising law, but it can be difficult to ascertain from them what they enjoy. It's worth your while persisting with getting to the bottom of their motivational needs. Getting to the bottom of your motivational needs would help in the process of engaging with the people you lead. If you can reveal to them more about yourself, you can model the process and they are more likely to respond. The problem I find with this process working with legal teams is the extent to which lawyers within teams are antagonistic to each other. It doesn't take long before they are channelling their inner litigator. I have spent more time than I would have liked in one-to-one sessions with members of legal teams who focus on criticising their colleagues – sometimes with good reason, sometimes not. Apart from those GCs who are naturally good at creating thriving environments – and I find these are mainly, but not always, women – I struggle to persuade some GCs and heads of legal to take a more empathetic approach. I'm hoping this book will help to persuade them that, in the long term, they and their legal teams and their employer clients and society will have better outcomes if they encourage rather than shame. Shame and shaming are ubiquitous in legal leadership and are the enemies of personal and team growth and performance. Those GCs interested in sport may be swayed by the evidence that coaches with an empathetic approach to their team members have more success over the longer term.

3. Developing the legal function

The next objective of a leader is growth and development against whatever metrics are agreed within the organisation. This is problematic for in-house lawyers – save those with natural flair in this area – since their bosses are not lawyers and can't make an accurate assessment and since lawyers are often not always skilled in developing functions and in reporting on that development. In Chapter 7, I propose a framework that GCs can use to help solve this problem. Meanwhile, the headline to bear in mind is to hyper-communicate the link between the PSB of the legal function and that of the employer client. By 'hyper-communicate', I mean just that: keep repeating, using every channel possible – email, monthly updates, phone calls, seminars, presentations and, especially, in-person catch-up meetings with key people on the executive and, if possible, the main boards – how the legal function's PSB is linking with the organisation's PSB.

4. Meeting stakeholders' needs

Finally, a leader must meet all stakeholder needs, not just those of the most powerful. In the case of in-house lawyers, the most powerful stakeholder is their employer client. The other stakeholders of the legal function include the court, society, employees, customers and suppliers. In an ESG environment, these needs are increasingly important; but I acknowledge that the motivation for prioritising the needs of stakeholders other than the employer client is difficult for in-house lawyers because their client is also their employer. This tension is addressed at length in Chapter 6.

5. Decision-making steps

In-house lawyers have an opportunity to take the lead in setting the

The three leadership components set out above – creating an environment in which people thrive, developing the legal function and meeting stakeholder needs – form the foundation for good decision making by all leaders, lawyers or not, on teams and boards.

standards for good governance on boards by modelling excellent decision-making behaviour in their legal function teams and within the in-house profession. Their internal value could soar accordingly at a time of emphasis on ESG. Boards are struggling to weave these new factors – increasingly driven by so-called 'activist investors' – into their decisions. The three leadership components set out above – creating an environment in which people thrive, developing the legal function and meeting stakeholder needs – form the foundation for good decision making by all leaders, lawyers or not, on teams and boards. Behaviour in taking decisions has a critical impact on outcomes. 'Conduct' is defined as behaviour over time. So poor conduct in decision making is a significant risk. In working with teams and boards, I recommend the following steps. Clients have found them useful. You can use these in your legal team meetings. If you are a GC acting as a company secretary or with a significant influence on board behaviour and governance, you might suggest these to your chair if they are not already in place.

5.1 Step 1: Share personal PSB plans
In my work with boards and teams, I have found that every team and board approach to taking decisions is unique because every team and board is unique because every member of that team or board is unique. Personal motivations trump governance systems. All the governance codes and decision-making models in the world are useless unless your legal team and employer client board members first share their personal purpose on the team or board – why they are there; their strategy or approach to being on the team or board; and their behaviour plan to implement their strategy to achieve their purpose, and especially how they feel that plan is going for them. You might think that organisational politics would dictate that many, if not all, of your legal team members or those of your employer client board members might not risk sharing this personal information; or that if they did, they might lie or partly lie. My experience in facilitating teams and boards is the opposite. I find that, if facilitated properly by a good leader with good skills or by a good facilitator, the incentive for team or board members to share deeply personal information is because they can see that the day-in, day-out pain of working on a dysfunctional board is so intolerable that they are willing to take personal risks. It

takes just one strong personality on your legal team or your employer client board to take the lead in sharing their personal story for others to quickly follow. If that one personality surprises colleagues with their candour, sharing will accelerate, as I experienced in one executive board facilitation where one member absolutely surprised their board colleagues with a deeply moving personal purpose story, after which others followed with their own stories, with a measurable impact on the decision-making culture of the executive board.

I acknowledge that some legal team and board cultures are so toxic due to the narcissistic behaviour of, usually, one bully that the process I suggest might seem naive. I urge you to wait to jump to this conclusion. First, there's a difference between a dysfunctional legal team or board and one that is driven by one bully. That's a different problem needing a different solution. Second, I find that teams and boards can get stuck in silo behaviour not because they want to do so, but because they don't know how or feel powerless to change the culture and because silo behaviour can feel set in stone. Finally, and most importantly, don't write off your team or board as beyond hope until you take the time to get to know each other. This ostensibly simple step, I find, can change the culture of a team or board in a surprisingly short period. This is because, as Warren Buffet's associate Charlie Munger famously advised: "Never, ever think about something else when you should be thinking about the power of incentives."[1] He was not referring just to financial incentives. Lawyers as leaders need to consider soft incentives for those they lead. The incentive for a team or board member to risk sharing their personal story – or, in the words of Brené Brown, to "dare greatly"[2] – is that the assumed pain associated with the risk of sharing is much less than the pain of continuing with the status quo. I can tell within five minutes, and so can you, if a team or board know each other as people with lives and stories outside work. If they don't, you can immediately see that their decision-making behaviour suffers accordingly, leading to personal fulfilment/wellbeing, organisational and societal risks. The legal team can model this behaviour for its employer client board, thereby enhancing its internal value.

5.2 Step 2: Agree on an organisation or team PSB plan
If the purpose of your employer client board is to maximise profits and nothing else, it should admit that, take responsibility for it and judge its decisions against that benchmark. If on the other hand, the board wants to balance profit with ESG issues, it should not merely pay lip service to those issues – it must agree upfront to what extent ESG will figure in its decisions. Equally, the PSB plan of your legal function needs to be shared by you and all your colleagues in your legal function. I believe that purpose is to enable employer client strategy through excellent legal counsel and process in the service of creating a sustainable organisation, considering the environment and society. But that's my definition; and the role and purpose of the legal function are explored in more depth elsewhere in this book. What's important is that your legal function has an agreed PSB upon which to base its decisions. Part of your legal function strategy to achieve your legal function's PSB could be to influence your client board to ensure that good governance in the service of the environment and society is part of its purpose. What if your legal function could model this PSB behaviour? If it could, I believe its internal perceived value would soar within the organisation – primarily as the ESG and sustainability movement gathers pace, as I'm certain it will. I acknowledge, for reasons discussed in Chapter 6 that – unlike other functions in organisations – the role and purpose of the legal function have not, over the years, settled down into an agreed statement across business and the legal profession. Nevertheless, you and your legal colleagues will have more fulfilling day-to-day work lives, less stress and a greater positive impact on your employer client if you and they take the time to agree a consensus on your legal function PSB statement – even if it is not perfect and even if it is not shared throughout the profession. If you can influence your employer client to do the same, your perceived value will increase.

5.3 Step 3: Agree on a board or team PSB plan (ie, terms of reference)
This is a different step from agreeing on an organisation PSB. It's a short step, but an important one. It's about the terms of reference of the team or board. What is its purpose? Its strategy? Its behaviour plan? For example, one executive board with which I worked had no terms of

reference and no clarity on its purpose and so relatively unimportant decisions appeared on the agenda, consuming valuable time and causing endless frustration among those who wanted serious matters given time at board meetings. In addition, important matters which required debate first at committee level were brought to the executive board without any groundwork done. Worse, some matters were debated at length at committee level and were brought directly to the main board, bypassing the executive board altogether. These problems were easily fixed because there was a will on this particular executive board to fix them. The executive board agreed on its purpose and on its terms of reference. That board's PSB, if you like. Of course, on other boards, I find that it may suit some to dilute the power of all boards or committees so that decisions are taken by a few people away from the board or team. Board meetings become a sham. The rationale usually offered for this behaviour is that "We'll get nothing done if we go through the motions"; or "The NEDs are muppets so let's crack on"; or "Meetings are a waste of time – so I'll decide." Take your pick. I understand how some leaders find that they are not matched in ability by some of the people on their boards and teams, and/or find procedures which they can't change cumbersome and frustrating. The problem with that argument is that it is a cake-and-eat-it approach, as I found once on a *pro bono* board on which I sat where the decisions were stitched up in advance by the chair and the CEO. This works while all goes well; but I found that when the air cover of perceived collective responsibility was required by the board, then it was consulted – or used and abused, in my view. I resigned. I advise you as an in-house lawyer – in your role as advocate of good governance – to respect boards and committees always, even when they are frustrating. You can and should be an agent of change in addressing the frustrations by being a supporter of old-fashioned standing orders – proposing motions, seconding them and voting – because these good governance processes are a bulwark against risk of the domination of one voice. This happened with Tony Blair, who otherwise was in my view a good prime minister; but he did succumb to the dangers of sofa decision making, as famously criticised in *The Chilcot Report*:

> *Tony Blair's "sheer psychological dominance" played a key role in the run-up to the Iraq war and meant that flawed evidence justifying the*

2003 invasion was never challenged, Sir John Chilcot told MPs on Wednesday. Giving evidence to a parliamentary committee, Chilcot said "sofa government", in which ministers were not consulted on crucial decisions, reached a high point under Blair. This reflected Blair's personal preferences, he said. He said that on several occasions between 2002 and 2007 "things were decided without reference to cabinet". They included the legal basis on which the UK went to war in 2003 as part of a US-led coalition and the decision, once Saddam Hussein had been toppled, for Britain to take over the administration of four of Iraq's southern provinces. Referring to the evidence given to his inquiry, Chilcot said he recalled asking the then foreign secretary, Jack Straw, why the cabinet had not "provided more of a challenge" to Blair or demanded more information. "The answer that came back was that Tony Blair had, as leader of the opposition and in government, rescued his party from a dire predicament. I had the sense from Straw's answer that he had achieved a personal and political dominance, a sheer psychological dominance.[3]

5.4 Step 4: Agree on a decision-making process

If your legal team or employer client board does not act in a collective decision-making sense, what's the point of the team or board? Why pretend it is a board or team decision when the decision is made by the GC on the legal team board or the CEO on the employer client board? You may argue that that is the reality of business life, and that my views are not realistic – not in tune with the *realpolitik*. You may be right; but I urge readers to find a midpoint between capitulating to the status quo of office politics and belief in an unrealistic nirvana. That mid-point is realistic and can be found by negotiating small changes in decision-making behaviour with colleagues. I have witnessed this approach working well. Agreeing a decision-making process can take the heat out of the meeting and shed much light. Old-fashioned standing orders have their place: speaking through the chair, proposing and seconding motions and voting. On big issues, don't forget to vote – even if it's not a formal or legal vote. This stops people hiding. It prevents the loudest voice from driving decisions. Your decision-making process might look like this: one member of the team formally proposes a decision which

How many meetings have you attended during which you remained silent about an issue or behaviour on which you felt strongly? How many times did you stand by and watch a colleague be bullied or wronged and didn't speak up? How many times did you witness hard work go uncelebrated?

includes by when and by whom action notes. Ideally, the motion should be seconded by another team or board member. The proposer makes an explicit link between their proposal and the shared team and organisational PSB, assuming this has been shared and agreed previously. The rest of the team give their views. Around the table, there is no hiding. No silences. Everyone must express a view. A vote is taken – a show of hands is fine – and the decision is recorded. Then everyone backs the decision or resigns.

5.5 Step 5: Appoint a devil's advocate by rotation at each meeting

How many meetings have you attended during which you remained silent about an issue or behaviour on which you felt strongly? How many times did you stand by and watch a colleague be bullied or wronged and didn't speak up? How many times did you witness hard work go uncelebrated? Which business decisions did you disagree with, but didn't feel able to fight? One way of alleviating these problems is to appoint or ask for the appointment of a devil's advocate by rotation at each meeting who is permitted – nay, expected – to say the unsayable, speak truth to power and challenge every critical decision. The GC in a legal team or the chair or CEO on a board could never act as devil's advocate; but every other team or board member should be required to take on the role by rotation at each meeting. The process would not change how you conduct the meeting or who speaks when or how, save that at the end of the meeting, the devil's advocate for that meeting would speak without interruption or challenge. For example:

Chair, you spoke over Joe Bloggs several times during the meeting. Joe Bloggs, you allowed yourself to be spoken over. This behaviour is unsustainable and poor governance. No one spoke up on Item 4 when we all know it's a controversial issue, and I have heard colleagues debate this issue hotly outside meetings. We must revisit this issue. On Item 12, we spent no time planning how to celebrate the behaviour of that function, which was odd given how much the results from that function have improved. Unless we celebrate successes, we won't motivate the teams and therefore reduce the chances of achieving our objectives.

And so on. The point of the devil's advocate is to ensure that what's said outside the meeting – usually the best commentary – is said inside the meeting, safely.

"No chance," I hear you say, "of this happening on my team or board." If true, then expect next year's decisions on your team or board to be as good or as bad as last year's. Team and board decision making reminds me of the film *Sliding Doors*. The film presents two outcomes. In one, the main character just about makes it through the closing doors of a train and the outcome is X. In the other, they don't, and the outcome is Y. Catching the train was, therefore, a 'sliding doors' moment. The movie dramatises the two alternate outcomes, popularising the expression: "a sliding doors moment." It's a powerful image. Team and board meetings are like that film. Decisions are taken or not. Discussions are had or not. People speak up or not. The implications of these alternatives are grave. The stakeholders who suffered because of corporate scandals will know how grave. NEDs can help if they act as critical friends of the business. But the power of NEDs is limited by how much information they receive, their courage and the board's culture. Worryingly, some NEDs tell me that they have influence but no power, despite the power they hold under the Companies Acts. They have power but don't use it. So, what to do? You can do nothing, and nothing will change; or you can decide at your next team or board meeting that you want to put processes in place to reduce these risks to your business. The cause of company failure or significant risk events will be in the decision-making processes. I suspect, if done correctly, the team or board would reverse or amend many vital decisions using the devil's advocate process. Fundamental issues affecting the future of the business – primarily conduct risk – would be called out. Your devil's advocate would require a mandate to represent all stakeholders – not just shareholders and the banks, but creditors, large and small, employees, their families, the environment and society.

Larry Fink, CEO of BlackRock, has said repeatedly that "society is demanding that companies, both public and private, serve a social purpose". Financial journalists frequently write that board members of organisations in trouble did not ask the right questions, and that carrying on as before has already led to a fractured society. Merryn Somerset Webb, the editor in chief of *Money Week* – not exactly a left-leaning newspaper – has opined that since "most adults in the UK have a stake in the listed UK sector, they should know that – be able to act upon it". The *zeitgeist* is changing. Women are standing up to predatory men at work. Electorates are defying old voting patterns. Investors see the writing on the wall for old processes. They see that the current model isn't working. They also know that it's not a binary solution – capitalism versus socialism – but a midpoint which gives all stakeholders a say in matters which affect them. Perhaps the term should be 'stakeholder advocate' and not 'devil's advocate'. But if these arguments do not persuade you to implement a devil's advocacy process at your board meetings, you might ask yourself why. Is it because you're afraid? If you are, then the seeds of self-destruction are already sown in your organisation. It's only a matter of time.

5.6 Step 6: Track the implementation of decisions

This is a short but critical step. Among my clients' top seven frustrations is the failure to implement decisions agreed at meetings, instead revisiting them again and again unnecessarily only then to fail to implement them. A simple decision tracker system at weekly update meetings solves this problem.

5.7 Step 7: Review outcomes and learn from them

Learning from successes and mistakes is the next step. This step depends on the extent to which there is a culture in which mistakes are permitted or even encouraged. The best sports coaches permit errors in their players. Indeed, they punish only those who don't take risks. They avoid shaming. So, what key decisions did your legal team or main or executive board make last year? How many were good? How many bad? How can your team or board avoid repeating the errors of last year? Can you all agree on what constitutes a good or bad decision? If your board decided to fire X, hire Y, spend A, not spend B or launch C, are you sure you know who on your team or on your employer client board agreed with those decisions and who didn't? Did everyone vote? Did your CEO decide? Did your chair hold sway? Did your CFO stop your CEO in their tracks? Were you or your GC in the room? Might any of last year's decisions land your organisation in legal trouble or onto the front pages next year? Against what benchmark were those decisions judged – short, medium or long term? Were the decisions based on financial criteria only? Were ESG issues taken into account? Who on your board is holding a silent and bitter grudge against a decision taken last year? Who has left your business who could damage it later? Do you know? If not, why not? Even if the most forceful personality on your board took the decisions and you were too scared to speak up, does that person have anything approaching a decision-making process? How might your legal team, main or executive board make better decisions?

6. The FRC code on decision making

The FRC Governance Code 2018[4] and Guidance on Board Effectiveness[5] are useful decision-making tools for any team or board large or small, listed or not. They ask good questions on this issue:

> *Questions for boards*
> *Have relevant members of the executive team been invited to explain the issues at the earlier stages, enabling all directors to share concerns or challenge assumptions well before the point of decision? Does the board have a clear idea of the success criteria related to a particular decision? What are we doing to test key decisions for alignment with values? Can we give examples and explain how this was considered? What are the risks that the decision could encourage undesirable behaviours or send the wrong message? Can we explain how the impact on key stakeholders has been taken into account?*[6]

7. Challenging behaviour: from bullying to martyrdom

Bullying was Margaret Thatcher's outstanding behavioural weakness at work, and it brought her down. Thatcherism and bullying were synonymous. Her operating model included bullying as an essential process in the execution of her plans. I use the word 'bullying' deliberately. It means being cruel. She was, at times, very cruel. Many of her lieutenants were afraid of her. This occurs in business and sport as well as in politics. Many people I know are terrified of their bosses.

But leadership by fear lasts only for a short time. Sooner or later, the terrified will find a way of fighting back. That said, Margaret Thatcher and all those given to bullying do so because they see no other way of behaving. For them, there is no midpoint between bullying and being bullied. Often, they were bullied at home and/or at school. You can read many books and articles on how to deal with bullying. My preference is to join forces with others and tackle the bully head on. If you can't do that, leave. I learned the power of lining up forces against bullies in my first year at boarding school.

We were 12/13-year-olds away from home for the first time at a time when boarding schools in Ireland had draconian views on contact time with home. There was one visit from family allowed per term and the terms were long. The Christmas-to-Easter term was notorious: long, cold and miserable. We were effectively prisoners, and our captors were more the older boys than the teachers. Many of the older boys, especially the second-year students, made our already miserable lives more miserable. There were five big lads in second year who made our lives dreadful and one day in Religion Class, Brother Y – a nice man – somehow managed to get us talking about the behaviour of the second years towards us. After hearing our tales of woe, he said: "Why don't you all put their names in a hat and I'll sort them out?" "That would be 'squealing'" – the Irish word for 'snitching' – we said. "Yes," he said, "but they wouldn't know who." Balancing the pain of ongoing horrors with the fear of retribution, we choose to whistleblow, *en masse*. The impact was swift, electric and most satisfying. The following evening, the principal marched noisily to the front of the study hall and made a brief speech about having zero tolerance for bullying. He then called out the names of the five and asked them to stand up. He told them their parents would be called and that they may be expelled; but in any event, that the bullying would stop. It did. Bliss.

If you're a bully or if you bully sometimes – we all can bully sometimes – check in with what frightens you. Ask for help. Use Feel/Need/Do (see Chapter 1) as a tool to connect with what you feel and need. Usually bullies – apart from psychopaths and extreme narcissists – are frightened people who are not self-aware, lack empathy and struggle to negotiate their needs productively. The components of EQ (see Chapter 2) are key to navigating our relationships. We all have strengths and weaknesses in our EQ. The latter are remedial if we first accept them without shame.

While bullying is the most quoted challenging behaviour at work, there are others. Passive aggression – the masking of hostility – and silence are two common techniques used as tools of control. Micro-management – a sign of problems with trust (see Chapter 2 for a case study) – is common among leaders, including GCs. Martyrdom by team members is less common but noticeable when present. In Ireland, we say, "There's a fierce smell of burning martyr in this room." Hubris – excessive pride – can kill an organisation and has done so to many. Finally, informality can lead to poor corporate governance and major risk events, as discussed earlier.

Which of these do you observe in your team on your board? What can you do about them? The key is to change yourself first – just small changes: if you're a bully, bully less by trying to understand why you bully. If you are passive-aggressive, risk occasional confrontation; note that you don't die. If you usually remain silent, try speaking up and see what happens. If you micro-manage, agree a 'soft' contract with a colleague to reduce your micro-managing behaviour in exchange for them changing their behaviour. If you're a martyr, treat yourself to a period of doing nothing. If you suffer from hubris, stop it. If you tend towards informality in meetings, try old-fashioned standing orders and see the difference.

8. Points of inflection on boards

In my mind's eye, as I write, I recall the main and executive boards I have facilitated over the years, the typical contexts in which I facilitate boards through change and the contexts in which in-house lawyers deliver their legal counsel and process:
- the first 100 days of uncertainty caused by a new CEO, chair or directors;
- matters arising following a board evaluation or negative employee survey;

- stress on relationships in rapid growth phases, especially after a funding round;
- transition issues post-merger, acquisition or new ownership, demerger or employee ownership trust;
- the need for improved decision-making behaviour and less silo behaviour on a board;
- the need to agree on a shared and common PSB; and
- culture change required to include ESG criteria in decision-making behaviour.

These points of inflection unsettle everyone and create risks, mainly conduct risks. CEOs, chairs, and executive or NEDs need help settling into new roles. Members of their main or executive boards need help to frame their relationship with the new board member. They also find that they must reframe their relationships with their colleagues, which will almost certainly change because of the new person. Board effectiveness reviews or evaluations or employee surveys can raise questions relating to the behaviour of members of your employer client board – particularly in their decision-making behaviour. The relationships on your employer client board can change dramatically due to pressure to deliver results following a funding round. The politics on your board will have shifted. Relationships on your board will come under significant strain if your organisation has merged, demerged, been acquired or restructured significantly. If your employer client is a family business and, for example, one member of the family has stepped up to a more senior role on your board, that transition significantly impacts relationships between family and non-family board members. Your employer client board members may be operating in silos, acting as if they are on their own, afraid to challenge each other at board meetings for fear of treading on each other's toes. Their board meetings may be heavy on updating, light on decision making. Above all, in my experience, your employer client board members may not all share a common PSB plan. Latterly, your board may struggle to incorporate ESG thinking into its decision-making processes.

If I were working with your board during one or more of these typical contexts, I would be working with the members of your main or executive board or both, and with the GC. They usually sit on executive boards and frequently act as company secretaries on main boards. My approach is to explore the interdependence of the personal PSB plan of each member of the board, including the GC, and the PSB of the organisation. For every board, performance improvement is about improvements in its decision-making processes – that is, governance – which requires behaviour change. This requires a reframing of relationships by surfacing personal motivations and feelings about each other. So my process is to have one-to-one sessions with each board member – including the GC – to understand their personal PSB; followed by plenary sessions of the board, often in an off-site setting; followed by another round of one-to-one sessions; and then as many plenary sessions required to sign off on soft behaviour contracts between members of the board in which they agree to make small changes in their behaviour (see earlier chapters on what I mean by and examples of soft behaviour contracts).

In my one-to-one sessions, I ask each board member, including the GC, the following questions:
- "What do you think the purpose of your organisation is and do you feel that that purpose is shared by all on the board? Ditto its strategy and behaviour plan?"
- "What is your personal purpose, your career objective? Why are you here?"
- "How are you going about achieving your personal purpose and do you have a plan for implementing that strategy?"
- "How is it all going for you? What's going well on the board? What's not?"
- "Which relationships on your board are problematic and why?"

Usually, there are about eight to 10 members on a board; and after eight or 10 one-to-one sessions of up to two hours in length, I have a deep understanding about the extent to which organisational PSB is clear and shared, each person's PSB and – crucially – where the tensions lie on the board and between whom. It's against this background that you, as an in-house lawyer, do your work – whether it is at a process or strategic level, or both. It is in this context that serious problems occur.

These stress points can lead to changes in behaviour on boards and within teams, including the legal team. In these cases, you may find it useful, irrespective of your rank within the legal team, to keep a watchful eye on and, if possible, to influence these dynamics:

- Has your employer client's purpose changed and is it still shared by all? Has the purpose of the legal function changed in any way? Are there any shifts in emphasis? For example, nothing shifts incentives more quickly than funding rounds.
- Be alert to changes in the personal purpose and behaviour of those on your employer client board and on your legal team.
- Note the interdependence between personal purpose and organisational purpose. How will people get what they need and how will the business get what it needs from them? How can you contribute to creating an environment in which people on your legal team or employer board can thrive?

9. "Least Likely to Say ..." is a useful legal team or board game

"Least Likely to Say ..." is a useful game to play if you want to improve relationships on a team or board. It's easy to play and, although I facilitate these, you don't need a facilitator. Here are the instructions:

- **Step 1 – It:** Choose someone in the team to be 'it'.
- **Step 2 – Shout out:** Everyone else shouts out what they feel the person who is 'it' is least likely to say first thing on a Monday morning.
- **Step 3 – Repeat:** Repeat the process for everyone on the team or board.

It's hilarious. Examples of 'least likely to say ...' include:

- "No need to check in with me. Just crack on. I only need the odd email/call."
- "Sorry."
- "It's my fault."
- Anything
- "No."
- "Yes."
- "What do you think?"

- "Great idea!"
- "Well done!"
- "I'm tired."
- "I'm not tired."
- "Help."
- "I don't need any help."
- Swearing.
- Apologising for swearing.
- "I don't know the answer."
- "I know the answer."
- "I feel ..."
- "I'm not going to tell you how I feel ..."
- "I was wrong."
- "He/she was wrong."
- "I was right."
- "He/she was right."
- "That's unethical."
- "We can't do that."
- "I'm fine."
- "I'm not fine."
- "Everything is great at home."
- "Everything is terrible at home."
- "I read a great book."
- "I'll do that."
- "Can I help you with that?"
- "Sorry, I shouldn't have said that in that way."
- "Let's go to the pub."
- "Let's not go to the pub."
- "I'm giving up reading business books."
- "Let's fix, not point."
- "Does anyone disagree?"
- "Let's have a devil's advocate in the room on this decision."
- "I can't do that – I have a family thing on this weekend/this evening."

A client once turned the tables on me and played this game with me at a dinner. He said: "Ciarán is least likely to say: 'I don't care what people think about me.'" I blushed. For he was right – 'tis true. What are *you* least likely to say?

10. 'Small change' soft contracts

There is only one way to create an environment for sustainable behaviour change in your leadership team, and that is to agree on soft contracts between each member and to legislate for the breach of those contracts. By a 'soft contract', I mean an unwritten agreement between two members to change the behaviour called out by the other a minimum of 10 times in every 100 interactions. That's just 10% change. Small change. But small change is hard to do. The incentives to try are as follows:

- It's good for you because the other party agrees to change their behaviour towards you;
- It's good for you because of the aggregate impact of the small changes on the team; and
- It's good for your organisation, for obvious reasons.

Here are three case-study experiences:

- A micro-managing CEO agreed to micro-manage by at least 10% in return for an accountability-shy marketing director admitting to mistakes 10% more (see Chapter 1, section 7 for a detailed account).
- A director agreed to back his colleague openly at meetings on matters he supported outside of them, and in return his colleague would no longer refuse to share his business contact list with him to help him build his network.
- A director agreed to say less – or at least think twice before speaking – at meetings in return for his leader confronting their behavioural issues.

It's important to legislate for the breach of these soft contracts, because they will certainly be broken: people are fallible and ingrained behaviour change is difficult to achieve. By 'legislating for the breach', I mean agreeing on specific actions in the event of a breach. For example, in the case of the micro-managing CEO, the arrangement was

– from memory – that the other party would ask him out for a drink to address the breach and to re-contract. It is possible for people to agree on these soft contracts without external facilitation. However – and while it's self-serving of me to say so, it's nevertheless true – facilitated soft-contracting has a better chance of success – not least because the facilitator, if they're any good, will be able to help the parties connect with why they behave the way they do. Do you know what annoys other people about your behaviour and its origin in your formative years?

Notes

1 Mental Models, "The power of incentives: The hidden forces that shape behaviour", Farnam Street, https://fs.blog/bias-incentives-reinforcement/.
2 Brené Brown, *Daring Greatly: How the Courage to Be Vulnerable Transforms the Way We Live, Love Parent and Lead*, Penguin Life, 2015.
3 Luke Harding, "Blair's 'psychological dominance' key in UK entering Iraq war, says Chilcot", *The Guardian*, 2 November 2016.
4 FRC Governance Code 2018, www.frc.org.uk/getattachment/88bd8c45-50ea-4841-95b0-d2f4f48069a2/2018-UK-Corporate-Governance-Code-FINAL.pdf.
5 FRC Guidance on Board Effectiveness, www.frc.org.uk/getattachment/61232f60-a338-471b-ba5a-bfed25219147/2018-guidance-on-board-effectiveness-final.pdf.
6 *Ibid.*

Chapter 6: Your client is your employer – how to manage that tension

1. Introduction

In this chapter, I set out the problems resulting from the fact that your client board is also your employer and explore how employer clients and in-house lawyers alike contribute to that problem; and I outline steps you might consider taking to deal with this issue. I have worked with hundreds of in-house lawyers. I use the same principles, tools and models to help them manage their relationships better as I do with those who are not lawyers to help them, especially with stress – stress about workload, relationships at work and ethical pressure. I feel lawyers are the closest we have left to guardians of morality, sanity and safety from moral hazards to us all in business. So, I feel simultaneously concerned and frustrated with in-house lawyers who sit on a spectrum between pain and complacency. The case I'm making in this chapter is that there is an opportunity for every in-house lawyer to reframe their relationships so that they can lead more rewarding and fulfilling careers, serve their clients more strategically and society more fully, and mitigate the risk of being unprepared for changes when they come. They can, I believe, find more peace and even joy at work than many do.

2. The problem

I find in my consulting practice that there can be a chasm in the relationship between in-house lawyers and their employer clients. Employer clients appear to me to be oblivious to the struggles of the in-house profession but crystal clear on what they expect from their employee in-house lawyers; and in feedback to me, they focus mainly on whether they are getting their needs met from their lawyers as they see them, or not. The most compelling evidence of this chasm between perspectives was a letter of complaint referred to as the "GC Response to SRA In-house Solicitors Thematic Review"[1] and signed by 33 GCs in the United Kingdom and sent on 23 March 2023 to the SRA and posted on social media.[2] The letter was a response to the *In-house Solicitors Thematic Review*[3] which the SRA had published on 14 March 2023. The response by the signatories was unprecedented. It marked the end of a period of what one in-house lawyer client called the longstanding *omertà*-esque silence among in-house lawyers about their situation; and what another described as an unwillingness to go, as he put it, "tall poppy". Well, tall poppy they went; and they didn't hold back. The letter is set out in full in Appendix 4. The letter was in two parts: first, the feelings of the signatories about the review; and second, their call to action of the SRA. My focus is on the former.

3. Analysis of the problem

The signatories to the letter – practising and retired GCs – were both among the most influential in the United Kingdom at the time and some not so influential: a cross-section of the in-house profession and the academics to whom they referred in their letter, global leaders in their field. The language of their feelings, which I extract below, was unambiguous about the seriousness, as they saw it, of the impasse:

> ... *leaders in the in-house legal community ... who have considered deeply the role of in-house lawyers and the positive impact they can have in society ... We are extremely concerned by the findings of the SRA In-house Solicitors Thematic Review. We are particularly troubled by the fact that the SRA does not appear to see the extent of*

the challenges for in-house solicitors that the Review signals ... the in-house legal community has significant influence and value, with 34,500 solicitors contributing to the growth and resilience of 6,000 organisations, and General Counsel serving an important leadership role in corporate decision making and risk mitigation ... a profession upon which so many rely and that has such a critical influence on the success and responsibility of our businesses and institutions ... independence is at the very heart of the tension in the client-employer relationship in-house and yet 64% of in-house solicitors are not raising their regulatory duties including the duty of independence with their client-employers ... One in ten experience pressure to compromise their regulatory obligations. 50% of General Counsel feel isolated. Many in-house solicitors are overwhelmed and have inadequate board support ... a matter for regulatory concern and action, not solely an issue for an individual solicitor to handle alone ... To have one in three in-house solicitors struggling to obtain sufficient resource to discharge their duties is a red flag that needs understanding and addressing ... It is also well established that financial pressures influence ethics and decision making and most would find it difficult domestically to accommodate a binary or subtle decision between enabling a course of action or resigning ... [an] opportunity to give the in-house legal working environment the attention it needs and deserves, and for which many in-house solicitors are desperate. There is much that is fantastic about the in-house legal world, but there are also systemic issues – as is the case in any sector. Identifying, acknowledging and tackling these head on has the potential to strengthen resilience and effective decision making within our corporations and institutions, help reduce corporate misconduct, and stimulate growth and a fresh approach into the future. With high profile cases such as the Post Office Horizon Scandal under review, and other corporate failings in the public domain including RICS, P&O Ferries, Rolls Royce, deferred prosecutions at banks, misuse of NDAs and more ... public trust in lawyers is both needed and in question ... support for General Counsel and in-house lawyers in the service of society, without the only choice being to resign or conform in conflict with professional and regulatory obligations ... strengthening the environment around in-house solicitors, to enable them to meet their professional and regulatory duties to their client-employers and wider society, and to not have to compromise their wellbeing along the way ...

This articulation of feelings reflected what academics and consultants – including me – had witnessed, written and spoken about over many years. For me, the letter was a great relief in terms of timing in writing this book, because for the first time I can use their words to support my observations of what is top of mind for them in their relationships.

4. What's top of mind for in-house lawyers?

Over many years, when I asked in-house lawyers what's top of mind for them outside of legal matters in their relationships, their responses have fallen under roughly seven headings which I feel capture the symptoms that reflect the malaise in their relationships, articulated so clearly in the letter to the SRA. The quality of those relationships is at the heart of the generic dysfunction in legal departments; and the solution, in part, lies in addressing the quality of those relationships under those headings:

- negativity towards legal departments;
- disrespect towards the legal profession, intellectual rigour and the law;
- ignorance of the law;
- ethical pressure on in-house lawyers;
- office politics;
- personal pressures, anxiety and stress; and
- tension between law departments and their employer clients.

4.1 Negativity
In their letter, the signatories refer to needing support in their 'working environment'. In this regard, negativity is the first symptom I hear in feedback – for example:

- "Why is your first answer always no?"
- "Your department is a cost, not a revenue centre."
- "You lawyers all think you're special."
- "Legal is slow to reply."
- "Legal brings problems instead of solutions."

This culture of negativity can be pervasive, relentless and sometimes nasty. Sceptics say that every non-revenue earning department attracts negativity. "That's business," they say. "Legal should suck it up," they say. Yet the negativity towards in-house lawyers seems to have a unique character separate from that experienced by marketing, HR, IT, finance and operations. It appears to reflect a feeling that in-house lawyers are not quite 'one of us'; that the lawyers know it and that they are desperate to feel the same as everyone else, but for reasons which are rarely explored.

Of course, the legal function has to say no regularly and cannot always offer easy solutions. That's its job. Lawyers are hired to advise their employer clients. Part of that advice must be to say yes or no in certain circumstances. So, why hire lawyers for advice if you are going to moan about it? But when you say no, it appears to be a different no from, say, an IT no or a Finance no. When an IT department said – to use an example I recall from my corporate career and have mentioned earlier in the book – that the board could not expect a system transformation to be in in place by its preferred deadline because it was impossible to achieve, for various reasons, the board was to be disappointed and annoyed, but the IT director was not told they were a blocker, as GCs are often told when they say no. Legal departments are cost centres, not revenue centres, like every other non-revenue generating department. So why the name calling?

The taunt of being 'special' is complex, not least because it's the last thing many in-house lawyers want to hear. They crave equality with the other departments. The problem is that they are special. They are different. They are regulated authorised persons with obligations beyond their employer clients. Sceptics claim that accountants are equally obligated. I disagree. Company accountants are not in the same regulatory bracket as in-house lawyers and don't owe exactly the same statutory obligation to society. It's noteworthy that accountants working within businesses are not called 'in-house accountants' and yet lawyers are called 'in-house lawyers'. Why? I feel it's because lawyers retain a sort of umbilical cord to private practice which gives them air cover and from which most of them came; and because

What can you, as an in-house lawyer, do about negativity?

businesses found it was cheaper and more productive to bring outside lawyers in-house. The term 'in-house' captures several layers of organisational schizophrenia. Finance directors would feel insulted to be called 'in-house accountants'. Yet GCs and their employer clients make no effort to discourage the use of the term.

Regarding inefficiency, it is of course true that some legal departments are inefficient and attract reasonable negativity for that reason. But again, even where this is the case, the tone of negativity used towards the legal function can be more vitriolic than towards other departments. IT might be derided in one business as 'hopeless' because of individuals within it, but the legal function can be marked down as 'hopelessly slow' not just because of individuals but because they are lawyers. Sceptics maintain that some lawyers are not resilient enough and should take this criticism on the chin. I'm not a fan of the word 'resilient' in this context. It's often used as code for 'man up' – a term, apart from its offensive gender connotations, that is used to conceal abusive behaviour. It places responsibility for the whole relationship back onto lawyers – an unreasonably one-sided demand. On the other hand, the use of the word to mean 'the ability to recover from difficult situations' is fine by me.

What can you, as an in-house lawyer, do about negativity? First, you can join and support those seeking regulatory support to improve your working environment. Second, you can emulate the signatories of the letter and express your feelings and needs more openly and regularly with your employer client. This requires courage. But you must be allowed to do your job; and if people in your organisation are making that difficult or even preventing you from doing your job, then you must call this out. Joining forces with colleagues, as the signatories did, can make this possible. You are not alone. Third, and as set out in more detail in Chapter 7, you can find ways of communicating your value to your employer client in a way that attracts more positivity.

4.2 Disrespect

The second symptom is disrespect of the profession, of the law and of intellectual rigour. Feedback includes, for example:

- "No one ever reads the contract."

- "Have you ever run a real business?"
- "We just need a short, simple agreement – it shouldn't be too hard ..."
- "The CEO won't let me do my job."
- "The NEDs are not supportive."
- "Often, I'm not invited into 'the room'."

Disrespect is different from negativity. Disrespect, according to my online dictionary, is about undermining another's position, status and value. Negativity is about relentless criticism and pessimism which I feel is tantamount to oppression. I felt so strongly about this issue that I gave a speech at a GC summit several years ago on the oppression of in-house lawyers. One in-house lawyer, carefully and in commendably restrained language, gave me the following written feedback:

> On oppression, it may be that [your] lead language causes a reaction that limits the ability of the audience to give the remainder of the message due consideration ... the language of oppression is reserved for slavery and other elements of serious abuse of human rights. This is not something that most lawyers would identify with applying to them and so an instant barrier can come up ... Most lawyers would also likely see themselves as individuals within a privileged elite rather than an oppressed body ... these absolutes work well with business people who operate in short-hand, for the detail-orientated lawyer they are a point to take exception to ...

I understand the feedback, but I have witnessed the oppression at close quarters in my work with clients. For me, the word 'oppression' captures how bad it can be for many, and that this oppression has become normalised. But since the word 'oppression' is not seen as in tune with in-house lawyers' identity, nothing is done. It has become increasingly clear to me over the years that while many in-house lawyers do suffer, it is not enough to get together and do something about it – until that letter written in March 2023.

You can help yourself and your colleagues find more respect and dignity in your work by coming together with your colleagues in your organisation and speaking openly – as the signatories to the letter did – about the challenge you face and emphasising your importance – as they did – of "a profession upon which so many rely and that has such a critical influence on the success and responsibility of our businesses and institutions". Educate your employer client leadership team on that critical influence. Confucius said, "Respect yourself and others will respect you." Equally, you must show respect to your employer client. Respect is a two-way street. Lawyers can exhibit ignorance of other functions – particularly marketing, with which department I have found lawyers appear to have a mental block. To repeat a story from earlier in the book: one equity partner in a law firm said to me in exasperation regarding marketing: "What's all this fuss about marketing? Surely all one needs is 40 tickets to Wimbledon?" That's not respectful.

4.3 Ignorance

The third symptom is one which dominates much of the feedback I receive – ignorance of the law and what lawyers do. Examples include the following:

- "They want to use their own paperwork but I'm sure it'll be fine ..."
- We didn't have an [anti-money laundering/market abuse/sanctions/ hedging policy] at my last place. Why do we need this policy?"
- "Our management consultant says it's legal."

I could have filled a page with these examples, but the above will suffice to illustrate the ignorance of the law and what lawyers do, which in-house lawyers experience daily. Ignorance is different from disrespect and from negativity. It's about lack of knowledge. It's not that lawyers expect their employer clients to know the law. It's that they expect them to know that they don't know the law. They find this lack of insight maddening and ubiquitous. Why hire a professional if you believe you know better than they do?

I wonder whether part of the problem here is that maybe you sometimes play down your asymmetrical knowledge because you want to feel the same as everyone else in the organisation – businessperson first, lawyer second – as often encouraged at legal conferences? I encourage you to consider doing the opposite: to be unashamedly you, as emphasised by the signatories in their letter: you are "serving an important leadership role in corporate decision making and risk mitigation". Your employer client will remain ignorant of your importance unless you tell them and own your power fully as a regulated professional, practising law in-house.

4.4 Ethical pressure

The fourth symptom is ethical pressure. The signatories to the letter were clear on this issue:

> ... independence is at the very heart of the tension in the client-employer relationship in-house and yet 64% of in-house solicitors are not raising their regulatory duties including the duty of independence with their client-employers ... One in ten experience pressure to compromise their regulatory obligations. 50% of General Counsel feel isolated.

Their feelings are borne out by the typical feedback I receive – for example:

- "If we get caught it's just the price of doing business."
- "You are new to our industry where behaviour X is the norm ..."
- "The CEO marked my annual review down because of what I called out at the board meeting ..."
- "What you're concerned about will NEVER happen."

These examples reflect the most egregious cultures – not in all organisations, for sure, but very common in my experience – where ethical pressure on in-house lawyers is routine. While I have met GCs who have not experienced ethical pressure at all, my experience working with hundreds of in-house lawyers is that most become accustomed to walking an ethical tightrope daily. Some leave because they can't cope with the stress of the balancing act. Others are forced out. What I have found scary, on behalf of society, is the extent to which the ethical compass of in-house lawyers varies considerably from lawyer to lawyer. I believe this is a direct result of the absence of enforcement by regulators of regulations in respect of the provision of legal services in-house. If, as in the regulation of private practice law firms, there were regular reports in the legal press of the enforcement of regulations, I believe that a consensus on ethical behaviour of in-house lawyers would quickly emerge. In addition, employer clients would be incentivised to behave better towards in-house lawyers or lose them completely. Academic research bears out the need for change. In the *Mapping the Moral Compass*[4] (see also Appendix 1) report published by the UCL Centre for Ethics and Law as far back as 2016, the headline findings included that:

- 10% to 15% experienced elevated ethical pressure; and
- 30% to 40% sometimes experienced ethical pressure.

The authors also noted that:

> ... *a number of our interviewees suffered exposure to what the following interviewee termed the "shouty man syndrome". IHL24 wraps up, rather nicely, the desire to be seen to be adding value, to not being a deal blocker, as a "helpful" part of the team.*

There was no public outcry at the time; but some in the legal profession took exception to the report because of its categorisation of in-house lawyers in respect of ethics, as noted by Rhymer Rigby in the *Financial Times:*

> *A recent piece of research from University College London on in-house lawyers, Mapping the Moral Compass, has caused a stir in the legal community. It identifies four main ethical groups of in-house lawyers: the capitulators, the coasters, the comfortably numb and the champions. Perhaps unsurprisingly, some general counsel have taken exception to these characterisations.*[5]

One GC said at the time of that debate that:

> ... *there is frustration that the moral compass of in-house solicitors would be called into question ... In-house lawyers have a good understanding of the professional obligations on them and that those professional duties are a large part of the value they bring to the*

company. Yes, they are dealing with just one client, the business, the whole time and they may be dealing with some ethical issues as well as legal issues – those ethical aspects are not only the purview of lawyers in companies by any means – but if you're alluding to this suggestion that there's some ethical difference between in-house lawyers and lawyers in private practice, I don't agree with that ...[6]

So, it was clear even then – and with sceptics now – that whatever ethical pressure in-house lawyers are experiencing, there is no groundswell of opinion that they should be treated any differently from private practice lawyers, or that their employment contracts could potentially frustrate their ability to act with independence. The fact that there are well-established procedures to address tensions between lawyers and clients in private practice but not in-house did not drive debate for change. There was and is a mixed appetite for additional regulatory support, even as the numbers of in-house lawyers increase; and to date, there has been no material change to the regulatory context in which in-house lawyers operate in the United Kingdom. One GC said to me: "I have a huge dislike for regulation being a free marketeer, but an absolute and respected right to whistle blow."

This dislike for regulation was illustrated when an attempt to include in-house lawyers in the Senior Managers Regime (SMR) in the financial services sector was squashed in 2019:

Firms, in-house lawyers and the legal profession generally will be relieved that the Financial Conduct Authority ("FCA") has decided to exclude firms' Heads of Legal from the requirement to be approved as a Senior Manager under the Senior Managers Regime ("SMR"). The FCA concluded that because so much of a Head of Legal's work relates to legal advice, the laws of legal professional privilege ("privilege") would likely restrict the FCA, in practice, from using its powers over Senior Managers. The benefits that normally result from applying the SMR will be substantially reduced so that any remaining benefits are not sufficient to justify applying it. However, Heads of Legal will continue to have to be certified by firms under the Certification Regime and be subject to the Individual Conduct Rules.[7]

This decision to exclude in-house lawyers from the SMR prompted a robust response from academics Clark, Moorhead, Vaughan and Brener, in a paper titled "Agency over technocracy: how lawyer archetypes infect regulatory approaches: the FCA example":

We have shown how the FCA's decision to exclude the head of legal from the SMR was based on a view of lawyers which is flawed. It is defective both from a theoretical perspective, since it portrays in-house lawyers as neutral legal technicians, who should be unaccountable for their conduct, and from a practical standpoint, since it fails to comprehend the significant levels of responsibility and influence in-house lawyers actually carry in regulated organisations in the financial sector. In squandering this opportunity to reinforce the ethical infrastructure of regulated organisations in the financial sector through the strengthening of the independence, authority and influence of in-house.[8]

It's clear to me that in-house lawyers are not better regulated because a majority have not demanded it, yet. But society, business and individual lawyers need you and your colleagues to be better regulated – as expressed at least by 33 of the 34,000 in their letter. Many fear reprisals if they speak out.

In respect of this fear of reprisal among in-house lawyers, Professor Stephen Mayson wrote, in his report *Reforming Legal Services – Regulation Beyond the Echo Chambers – Final Report of the Independent Review of Legal Services Regulation*:

As we have seen in recent years, corporate failures can lead to consumer and societal detriment. In-house lawyers have to be able to sound alarm bells without the chilling effect of potential reprisal. The public interest in effective and fearless legal representation is engaged in much the same way as it is in private practice ...[9]

Meanwhile, what can you do? My answer is simple: get behind those in your profession seeking change. You will benefit. All will benefit. You could also ask your employer client to add an amendment to your

The relationships between in-house lawyers in legal departments can be fraught. As fraught as any other department, for sure; but they are exacerbated by the fact that lawyers see themselves as individual micro-businesses forged in an adversarial crucible at law school and in their private practice training.

employment contract to acknowledge your regulatory obligations. In June 2022, ahead of the SRA's thematic review and response by the signatories to the letter, Jenifer Swallow – a GC and one of the signatories – and I published a template[10] contract amendment (set out in Appendix 3). We didn't have any uptake at the time, mainly because of the fears of in-house lawyers already explored in this book. However, I hope that as a result of the signatories going public and the work they have undertaken since, you might feel safer in raising the amendment with your employer client.

4.5 Office politics

The fifth symptom of dysfunction in-house is the impact of office politics on in-house lawyers. These are common to everyone working in an organisation. However, lawyers can struggle more than most with these because their training did not put a premium on soft skills. A sample of verbatim feedback includes:

- "The Group GC has gone native and won't listen to me ..."
- "My number two clearly wants my job, now."
- "Compliance is holding issues back from me."
- "X says the junior lawyer is being difficult rather than engaging on the business issue."

The relationships between in-house lawyers in legal departments can be fraught. As fraught as any other department, for sure; but they are exacerbated by the fact that lawyers see themselves as individual micro-businesses forged in an adversarial crucible at law school and in their private practice training. The relationship between GCs and their in-house legal teams can be particularly fraught if the GC lacks leadership skills and empathy, or has moved so close to their employer client that they have abandoned their independence. Succession planning is very difficult in in-house legal teams. Bright, ambitious lawyers can't move up until those above them move on. This frustration leads to increased tension and hostility, especially where one lawyer feels they would be the better GC. These tensions exist in all departments, but the difference is how the status quo relationships are managed by lawyers as opposed to those in other functions. Lawyers manage their relationships differently because of their training.

4.6 Personal pressures

The sixth symptom is the personal pressures and stress experienced by in-house lawyers just because they are in-house lawyers. The signatories of the letter refer explicitly to this problem: "It is also well established that financial pressures influence ethics and decision making and most would find it difficult domestically to accommodate a binary or subtle decision between enabling a course of action or resigning ..."

The feedback I have received supports this view:
- "You need to have a Plan B – you must have enough cash to afford to walk out ..."
- "I can't afford to walk out ..."
- "I lost my job for doing my job ..."
- "The stress of juggling demands is making my life miserable."

These comments represent the worst and most terrifying situations I have witnessed. What if you can't afford a Plan B? How can this be happening in a regulated profession? What is the profession doing about these nightmare scenarios which wreck lives? The answer is that these situations happen regularly and in plain sight. Lawyers are forced out of their jobs. Some sign non-disclosure agreements, some don't. In any event, society doesn't know that their officers of the court or authorised persons are being forced out of their jobs and staying quiet about it. And they are. If they are not forced out of their jobs, they feel they must leave them prematurely, leaving behind a mess for the next incumbent to perform the lawyer's version of the diving catch, again and again, until they have had enough and they too leave or are forced out. As mentioned earlier, the 'diving catch' is a cricket term whereby the player dives for the ball full stretch with no regard for the risk of injury on hitting the ground. Law school and private practice training is responsible for 'diving catch' syndrome because it teaches lawyers to do whatever is asked of them by their clients as quickly as possible. When lawyers go in-house, they continue this behaviour. If they don't deliver, they feel they have failed. In-house lawyers often work in this way without any regard for the risk of burnout, mental health issues and physical symptoms. One GC told me that it's not just the diving catchers who suffer. Their 'watchers' suffer too – that is, those who must helplessly observe the self-harm and the harm to those to those around them.

Their propensity for the diving catch explains why lawyers are so willing to do 'more for less' – a phrase which became popular at in-house lawyer conferences. The phrase refers to the belief that legal departments need to cut costs and add more value with less money. The implication was that they were doing less for more all along. "In-house lawyers will have to deliver more for less, survey finds," screamed a headline in the popular blog Legal Futures in June 2021: "Almost two-thirds of in-house legal departments are predicting increased workloads, despite most anticipating no increase in staff numbers and almost half expecting budget cuts, a survey has found."[11]

Thompson Reuters offered in its blog in September 2022, "Top 5 ways in-house legal teams can do more with less":

> There are several ways by which in-house counsel can successfully manage their corporate law department despite a reduction in overall resources & spending ... half of the senior in-house counsel surveyed cited "conducting operations in the most efficient way possible as a top priority for their law department, even more than safeguarding the business, which is arguably the main purpose of an organization's legal function".[12]

But in respect of budget management, Paul Gilbert – director of LBC Wise Counsel, a consultancy focused on supporting in-house lawyers – was giving them "tough love" in his blog as far back as 2013:

> Too many in-house legal teams are dark bottomless pits of inefficiency. Encouraged by faint praise they institutionalise a long-hours culture to manage workload, spectacularly missing the point that their ineffectiveness at managing demand might also have a part to play ... Instead lawyers tend to opt for requisitioning bigger buckets. The inability to manage workflow, while often at the same time as persisting in the fool's pursuit of proactively creating even

more demand is another demonstration of cock-eyed thinking. It is as if being "proactive" is an end itself. Being proactive is about as useful an ambition as ordering steak when you have no teeth ... Add in the fact that a great many of the in-house lawyer's external relationships with law firm suppliers lack governance, rigour and accountability and the picture is not even as positive as I have suggested.[13]

So, at one extreme, in-house lawyers are at pains to please their employer clients by doing more for less at any cost, including their mental health; and at the other extreme, there are highly inefficient in-house law departments, which also causes anxiety and attracts warranted criticism from their employer client. I have had experience of working with both extremes. In one instance, a senior in-house lawyer – clearly needing at least one additional lawyer to help them with their workload – was incredibly stressed by the demands, on that occasion, of three members of their employer client organisation all looking for work done by the same deadline. There seemed to be no communication with their GC on the problem. Just head down – more diving catch behaviour. At the other extreme, I worked with a GC who didn't know their law department's people costs. They did not know how many lawyers they employed and at what cost. They would have to look it up, they said.

These extremes are as staggering as they are understandable because lawyers are not trained to run efficient law departments. In fact, they are not trained to run anything. How can we blame them then when they fall short? However, there is one issue which they must take on the chin: many are invariably loath to tell, rather than ask, their employer client what it needs in terms of excellent legal counsel and process to achieve its objectives. Let's say the GC determines that the cost of achieving those objectives is $10 for 10 things and the budget they are given is $7; in my experience, many GCs will do 10 things for $7, with calamitous results in terms of the personal pressure on each individual lawyer in the department.

The current incentive is that their employer client will be pleased with them if they reduce costs. It appears not to matter that you might possibly know best how you can enable business strategy through delivering excellent legal counsel and process. Cost, not strategy, is the driver. Sometimes the problem is that lawyers don't understand strategy, are afraid to admit it and confuse a strategy with a plan. But again, why might we be surprised that in-house lawyers are under extreme personal relationship stresses and pressure when we expect them to achieve outcomes for which they were not trained?

The impact of these personal relationship stresses and pressures is incalculable. This excerpt from the International Bar Association website illustrates the point:

… Elizabeth Rimmer, Chief Executive of mental health charity LawCare, which focuses on prevention, education and support in the United Kingdom and Ireland, says significant research shows higher rates of anxiety and depression for lawyers across the board in comparison to the general public.

"There's something about the culture and practice of law having an impact on people – lawyers are the sort of people who are perfectionist and driven and find it hard to admit they are struggling," Rimmer notes. "At LawCare, the two most common reasons which contribute to lawyers feeling stressed are working long hours and difficult relationships with colleagues, where they don't feel well supported."

"They like to fix other people's problems, not their own, have a fear of making mistakes and the culture is very pressured, which can create the perfect storm," adds Rimmer.

Rimmer says in-house lawyers often are expected to work across a multitude of matters at the same time and to respond very quickly. "It can be tough trying to explain to the part of the business you might be supporting what the legal implications are of something they want done yesterday – and that you might be putting the brakes on that."

"People don't always understand what the legal function is and the pressure on lawyers in terms of delivering legal obligations; in a law firm, they'd get that, as everyone around is a lawyer," explains Rimmer.

Stresses start to mount at law school and in private practice training, where lawyers are not trained to prioritise relationships. They value what is measured. Some mythologise their training days. They recall their 'all-nighters' as rites of passage. They bury the negative consequences.

> *In-house lawyers in smaller organisations can feel isolated in a small legal team: "They may be sole counsel and not have colleagues who they can bounce legal things off."*[14]

These stresses start to mount at law school and in private practice training, where lawyers are not trained to prioritise relationships. They value what is measured. Some mythologise their training days. They recall their 'all-nighters' as rites of passage. They bury the negative consequences. So how can they best confront the fact that their legal training has not equipped them to value, develop and manage relationships in an organisational setting? It's one step to confront it intellectually, which they do with ease since they are all invariably bright. Doing so on an emotionally intelligent level is a different, tougher step, but one which can yield most benefit to them.

Lawyers are trained to focus on the details and to exploit small differences in litigation and contract negotiation. They are brilliant at ensuring not only that they win, but also that often the other side loses. Winning arguments is part of their identity. They often approach relationships with the mindset of winning an argument; so when they need to influence, persuade, and lead – which skills are at the heart of the in-house role – they can struggle.

Law firms cannot bill leadership by the hour. Law schools don't teach it. But leadership is a strategic resource in every business operating model – and legal departments are internal businesses with operating models. Lawyers' high IQs frequently cloak gaps in their knowledge and awareness of operating models. One senior in-house lawyer, when I suggested to him that the legal function should be run as an internal break-even business, replied: "I think that's too simplistic." Later I persuaded his organisation to adopt my operating model, but it took some persuading. I set out this model in Chapter 7.

Law departments need strong business leaders. Some organisations tend to promote the best lawyers but not necessarily the best leaders to GC roles. The following quote from Legal 500 *GC Magazine* Winter/ Spring 2020 edition, which captures some of these issues, was sent to me by a GC:

... according to psychologist (and former trial lawyer) Dr Larry Richard ... "Lawyers are the most atypical occupation on the planet. We are more different from the general public than any other occupation since data has been published. We are the original outliers," he says. Among 21 traits measured on a standard personality profile, Richard's research shows that lawyers' average scores for seven of these are dramatically atypical compared to the general public (it's considered unusual for even one trait to be atypical in most occupations). According to his research, lawyers score highest on scepticism, as well as on need for autonomy, urgency (read impatience) and ability for abstract reasoning. So far, so predictable, perhaps. But he also found that lawyers score low on sociability, psychological resilience, and cognitive empathy. Richard argues that scepticism is particularly encouraged at law schools, which, he says, attract candidates already predisposed to this trait and then train them to be even more so. "The training that we have as lawyers trains us to look for the negative. We are trained to look for problems, what could go wrong, what is wrong, what's not ok – we ignore the 95% that's working ... We're trained to be vigilant about hidden motives, what do you really mean by that, what's your agenda – it's that kind of hidden, almost paranoid mindset. All of these things make someone a very competent lawyer, because the better you can do these things, the more you're going to protect your client from a host of unseen potential problems," he explains. "But there is a price to pay and here's the built-in tension. All the other roles that we ask lawyers to play these days require just the opposite, because almost all the other roles are founded on relationships."[15]

The cost of this training, which poorly prepares lawyers for in-house roles, is exacerbated when we consider the tension in the relationship between in-house lawyers and their employer client organisations.

4.7 Inherent tension

The signatories to the letter make specific reference to tension inherent in their relationship with their employer client: "... independence is at the very heart of the tension in the client-employer relationship ..."

Their view is supported by Professor Stephen Mayson, who wrote in his Independent Review of Legal Services Regulation that "there is little doubt that a tension is inherent in this relationship when the client for legal services is also the adviser's employer".[16]

I've witnessed this tension at close quarters in my consulting practice. The cost of this tension is high. However, there appears to be no appetite – or indeed incentive – in the legal profession or in organisations to address this tension, even though both lawyers and organisations suffer high costs from the tension in personal terms and because of the potential for serious risk events. But society by far suffers most from this unresolved tension because it is usually the victim of corporate scandals, but it has no control over the relationship between in-house lawyers and their employer clients. Society appears powerless to address the underlying cause of the tension – possibly because, as in the case of many institutional scandals, it is not aware of the facts. Society is not aware that, over time, the independence of in-house lawyers has been eroded, and that their regulation and support have become light touch to the point of absence, despite the law on the provision of legal services.

The UK Legal Services Act 2007 states in its first section that "authorised persons should act with independence and integrity".[17]

In my day-to-day practice, I rarely – if ever – hear in-house lawyers refer to this line in the act, which gives them their mandate to practise. Indeed, when I raise this issue with them, many become irritated to be reminded of the law. Some feel I'm suggesting that it's not possible for lawyers to operate in-house – which I'm not. But when I ask them how they can possibly maintain their independence and avoid tension with their employer clients while having exactly the same employment contracts as everyone else in the organisation, they merely say they can, and they do; that they want to have the same contracts as everyone else and in any event, to suggest otherwise to their employer client would, as one GC put it, "be provocative". Another said: "... you don't need to be independent to sound alarm bells ... an understanding and respect for autonomy would suffice ..."

I agree with them that independence is not a prerequisite for sounding alarm bells. But contractual dependence on an employer client, with no reference to their regulatory obligations, surely does not create an environment for in-house lawyers to act with independence. Indeed, it increases the risks to society, to businesses and to individual lawyers – as borne out by anecdotal evidence, corporate scandals and academic research.

In this regard, Professor Stephen Mayson states in his report on in-house lawyers: "The usual expectation of 'independent' legal advice is often stretched ..."[18]

Richard Moorhead, Steven Vaughan and Cristina Godinho explore the issue in depth in *In-House Lawyers' Ethics – Institutional, Legal Risk and the Tournament of Influence*:

> ... *lawyer independence comprises at least four facets: first, being prepared to say 'No' to a client; second, an acceptance that independence may, in some situations, mean taking decisions that have negative financial consequences for the solicitor; third, a need for a solicitor to avoid becoming overly reliant or close to any given client; and finally, a recognition that, in litigation, individual lawyers are professionally responsible for their handling of cases (ie, they cannot simply rely on acting in accordance with the client's instructions to justify questionable tactics).*[19]

Feedback from in-house lawyers on regulation includes these comments:
- "Renewing a practising certificate is a joke, it's so easy ..."
- "We are, in real terms, not regulated ..."
- "If I were in trouble, I wouldn't call the regulator."

There is insufficient regulation or support from a regulator; and at the same time, the promotion, pay, bonuses, LTIPs and annual reviews are in the hands of their employer clients. How is that not a conflict? How can in-house lawyers subject themselves – as I know many do – to bell curve performance management systems administered by bosses who are not lawyers without sacrificing a considerable degree of their independence? How can it be that one GC was marked down in their annual review because they made reasonable challenges at board meetings? How can in-house lawyers with LTIPS deny that these plans might – note I say 'might', not 'would' – impact their ability to act with independence? Surely the word 'incentive' says it all. I know a few GCs who waived their LTIPs. They said that it made a significant difference to how they felt, behaved and were perceived on management boards. But these are a tiny minority. The main incentive for any change would be for regulators to support in-house lawyers to act with independence and to enforce the regulations as robustly in-house as they do out of house. Meanwhile, I believe that you, as an individual in-house lawyer, can make immediate changes if you apply even some of the ideas in this book which could make your working life much more fulfilling in the short and medium term, would serve your employer client better and would reduce societal risks.

5. Relationships in businesses

Relationships are at the heart of creating and destroying value in business according to A Blueprint for Better Business, a charity I have supported for many years. It sees business relationships as "the glue that inspires all of the people on which the business depends to succeed: its employees, customers, suppliers, the communities in which it operates, its investors and the future generations affected by what it does ..."[20]

However, the reality is that many businesses feel that contracts, not relationships, are at their heart. This creates a tension between business and society. We must accept this tension for the present if we are to have any hope of addressing it. Ironically, it is in-house lawyers who are tasked with drafting the set of contracts at the heart of business. In-house lawyers spend much of their time reflecting business relationships in contracts. In doing so, they are at the heart of what holds organisations together; and at the same time, because of the transactional nature of contracts and the protections required in them, in-house lawyers are to some extent necessarily part of a process which prevents organisations from creating an environment in which relationships can best thrive. It's no surprise, therefore, that they can sometimes fail to meet their own needs in the softer aspects of negotiating their own soft contracts. I define 'soft contracts' as the unwritten agreements between parties in a relationship as to how they agree to behave in that relationship, and particularly in relation to how each expects the other to change their behaviour and to legislate for the breach of those soft contracts. It's my contention that the unique problems facing in-house lawyers are linked to the fact that their soft contracts are not clear. In-house lawyers have many connections and therefore many relationships within their businesses and outside them. The quality of these relationships varies from lawyer to lawyer and business to business. In-house lawyers are not unique in experiencing problems in how they relate with others. But there are structural issues that make it more difficult for lawyers to address relationship problems. They also have advantages over others that they are, perhaps, not using to the full.

6. A new way

In-house lawyers who wish to make their working lives and careers immediately more fulfilling, improve their relationship with their employer clients and avoid the risk of being on the wrong side of the societal timebomb can do so only if they choose to reframe their relationships fundamentally and make small changes in behaviour which in aggregate will have a big impact on outcomes. That is subject of the final chapter.

Notes

1   Thirty-three signatories, *GC Response to SRA In-house Solicitors Thematic Review*, LinkedIn, 23 March 2023, www.linkedin.com/posts/jenifer-swallow-a1a4482_gc-response-to-sra-in-house-solicitors-thematic-activity-7044634751093071872-lF6_/?utm_source=share&utm_medium=member_desktop.

2   https://docs.google.com/document/d/e/2PACX-1vTsOgvh0qvOWK_kFXUUnqBct5bxHQuV3jzhDU9QwSbUUY59rJx4vjD1Pc5e9RSbZOt94emhyTrWNERS/pub.

3   www.sra.org.uk/sra/research-publications/in-house-solicitors-thematic-review/#:~:text=Our%20review%20showed%20that%20most,in%20retaining%20and%20recruiting%20talent.

4   Richard Moorhead, Cristina Godinho, Steven Vaughan, Paul Gilbert and Stephen Mayson, *Mapping the Moral Compass: The Relationships between In-House Lawyers' Role, Professional Orientations, Team Cultures, Organisational Pressures, Ethical Infrastructure and Ethical Inclination* (2 June 2016), https://ssrn.com/abstract=2784758 or http://dx.doi.org/10.2139/ssrn.2784758.

5   Rhymer Rigby, "In-house legal teams balance profit against morality", *Financial Times*, 21 June 2016, www.ft.com/content/c264c0d2-234e-11e6-9d4d-c11776a5124d.

6   Madeline Farman, "Lost in Translation", *Inhouse Lawyer*, Summer 2016, www.inhouselawyer.co.uk/feature/lost-in-translation/.

7   Stephenson Harwood, "Heads of Legal not required to be Senior Managers", February 2019, www.shlegal.com/docs/default-source/news-insights-documents/2019/e-alert—-heads-of-legal-not-required-to-be-senior-managers—-feb-2019.pdf?sfvrsn=3820115b_0#:~:text=The%20FCA%20concluded%20that%20because,its%20powers%20over%20Senior%20Managers.

8   Trevor Clark, Richard Moorhead, Steven Vaughan and Alan Brener (2022): "Agency over technocracy: how lawyer archetypes infect regulatory approaches: the FCA example", *Legal Ethics* 24(2):1–20, www.researchgate.net/publication/359771803_Agency_over_technocracy_how_lawyer_archetypes_infect_regulatory_approaches_the_FCA_example.

9   Stephen Mayson, *Reforming Legal Services – Regulation Beyond The Echo Chambers – Final Report of the Independent Review of Legal Services Regulation*, The Centre for Ethics and Law, University College London, June 2020, www.ucl.ac.uk/ethics-law/sites/ethics-law/files/irlsr_final_report_final_0.pdf.

10 www.jeniferswallow.com/posts/in-house-lawyer-independence-employment-amendment-letter.

11 Nick Hilborne, "In-house lawyers will have to deliver more for less, survey finds", Legal Futures, 25 June 2021, www.legalfutures.co.uk/latest-news/in-house-lawyers-will-have-to-deliver-more-for-less-survey-finds.

12 Irene Liu and Megha Sharma, "Top 5 ways in-house legal teams can do more with less", Thomson Reuters, 6 September 2022, www.thomsonreuters.com/en-us/posts/legal/in-house-legal-teams/.

13 Paul Gilbert, "The trouble with in-house lawyers", LBC Wise Counsel, January 2013, www.lbcwisecounsel.com/resources/articles/article/the-trouble-with-in-house-lawyers/#.Y3FEIuzP2Lo.

14 International Bar Association, "Mitigating wellbeing challenges for in-house lawyers", www.ibanet.org/article/b30bd02f-0d65-41df-99f9-fad7d3a8c2e4.

15 All in the Mind, "GC picks the brains of psychologists to uncover insights for corporate counsel to bear in mind …", Legal 500/*GC Magazine* Winter/Spring 2020 edition, www.legal500.com/gc-magazine/feature/all-in-the-mind/#:~:text=%27Lawyers%20are%20the%20most%20atypical,original%20outliers%2C%27%20he%20says.

16 Stephen Mayson, *Reforming Legal Services – Regulation Beyond the Echo Chambers – Final Report of the Independent Review of Legal Services Regulation*, The Centre for Ethics and Law, University College London, June 2020, www.ucl.ac.uk/ethics-law/sites/ethics-law/files/irlsr_final_report_final_0.pdf.

17 Legal Services Act 2007, Section 1(3)(a).

18 Stephen Mayson, *Reforming Legal Services – Regulation Beyond the Echo Chambers – Final Report of the Independent Review of Legal Services Regulation*, The Centre for Ethics and Law, University College London, June 2020, www.ucl.ac.uk/ethics-law/sites/ethics-law/files/irlsr_final_report_final_0.pdf.

19 Richard Moorhead, Steven Vaughan and Cristina Godinho, *In-House Lawyers' Ethics: Institutional Logics, Legal Risk and the Tournament of Influence*, Bloomsbury, 2019, pp90–91.

20 A Blueprint for Better Business, www.blueprintforbusiness.org.

Chapter 7: How to reframe your legal department's relationship with your employer client

1. Introduction

When I secured my first global GC client, I decided to pilot the relationship framework set out below. I had no previous experience of working with the top lawyer in an organisation with a large legal and support team across the world and one who reported to the CEO. I started – as I start every piece of work I do – with one-to-one interviews with as many people as I could: the group GC, the country GC, their legal team members, the CEO and their team, the risk people and so on. These interviews were time consuming but essential. In these I was first looking to understand the purpose, strategy and behaviour (PSB) plan of the employer client and the extent to which this was clear and shared throughout the organisation – particularly in the law department. Second, I was looking to understand whether the generic PSB plan of the legal function was clear and shared within the legal function and within the organisation, and that it linked transparently with the objectives of the organisation. Third, I was looking to understand the personal PSB plan of all the individuals involved, on the grounds that personal purpose and organisational purpose are interdependent.

The outcome of the interviews in this first case was the same as it has been in every case since. The purpose and strategy of the organisation are rarely completely clear; and if they are, they are not always shared by the executives at the top and certainly not always understood and shared throughout the legal department. The generic purpose and strategy of the legal function are similarly unclear to all – unsurprisingly, since this question is asked annually at legal conferences. Finally, personal purpose is not usually addressed at all; and even if it is to some extent, this is not systematic. But above all, the plan to implement the legal department's strategy to achieve its purpose in serving its employer client's purpose isn't always business-like. I felt then, as I do now, that there is no difference between the business of delivering excellent internal legal counsel and process and any other business. My problem was, and is, that – initially at least – I encountered and continue to encounter scepticism about the principle of running the legal function as a business. One senior lawyer said, again initially, that my approach was "simplistic". Another said that in-house lawyering is a Socratic process and that my approach was not appropriate. The purpose of this chapter, therefore, is to set out a relationship framework for the in-house legal function from which in-house lawyers can choose steps with which they initially feel comfortable to trial; and hopefully, in time, they may see the value to their own wellbeing of applying the whole framework, which doubles as a diagnostic tool.

2. Step 1: Secure a shared language on the PSB plan of your employer client

It's impossible for your legal function to function properly without securing a clear shared understanding of the PSB plan of your employer client. The legal function cannot decide what legal counsel and process to provide to its employer client if it doesn't know why the organisation exists, what strategy it has crafted to achieve that purpose and what behaviour or operational plan it intends to use to implement its strategy to achieve its objective. Yet many legal functions I encounter attempt to function without that clarity. Instead, they ask their employer client what it wants from the legal function, as if somehow the client knows everything about legal counsel and process. The legal function often judges itself on the extent to which it is seen as a business partner, as if the role and purpose of the legal function are to be a business partner. I've never understood that term and discourage its use. Many disagree with me, but few will deny that practising law is the legal function's core role. I'm not suggesting that it's easy to determine the employer client's PSB – not least because the employer client may not know itself, as is often the case. The PSB or operating plan of any organisation, you would think, should be clear and shared by those running it and working for it. The extent to which this is untrue is at the heart of many of the conflicts between people in organisations and between the legal function and its employer client. While your employer client may have set out its mission statement and values in its reception area, on its website, in press releases and in business plans, there can be a significant gap between reality and those aspirations. This gap can change over time and frequently depends on the whim of the person with the most power in the organisation. The real purpose, rather than the stated purpose, of an organisation need not be complex or lofty. It can be to maximise shareholder return and/or to make people's lives easier and/or to contribute to society and/or something else. Whatever the real purpose is, it must be clear and shared. By 'clear', I mean unambiguous. By 'shared', I mean that everyone on the main and executive board has explicitly agreed with the purpose, even if they have misgivings.

The first question I ask board members in my one-to-one sessions with them is to state their understanding of the shared purpose of the organisation. The range of answers can be shocking, from the parroting of the mission statement, often devoid of feeling, to woolly platitudes or to excellent clear statements accompanied by "but not everyone on the board agrees with me". The reason for this disparity is that the board members fail to agree on the interdependence between their personal purpose and the purpose of the organisation. The influence of personal purpose on organisations cannot be overstated. The evidence for this assertion is contained in the changes in purpose that occur when there is a change in CEO, prime minister or the top of a family business.

Strategy is not complex. It's merely how, in headline terms, a purpose is achieved. But a strategy is not a purpose and it's not a plan. It's how, in headline terms, the organisation will achieve its purpose.

In-house lawyers should check, therefore, the extent to which there is a clear PSB shared by the board and management team. The clearer and more widely shared the PSB, the easier will be the legal function's task. In-house lawyers can bring to their client's attention where there is a lack of clarity and to what extent they feel the PSB is not shared. At a time of greater, but uneven, emphasis on ESG, members of boards, executive boards and senior leadership teams can diverge from each other significantly on the impact of ESG on their purpose. For some, it's about making more money by appearing to care about ESG; for others, it's a genuine belief that society comes before profit and all viewpoints in between. These differing viewpoints can create problems for the legal function since many are asked to lead on ESG. So even if the PSB statement is less than perfect, try to secure one statement and feed it back in an email to the employer client so that there is no misunderstanding. In extremis, if you can't, after several attempts to secure a clear and shared PSB statement, I struggle to see how you can reasonably be part of a purposeful legal function in that organisation. Your relationships will have weak foundations. Growth and success of the type we are trying to promote here will be impossible. Frustration, stress and exhaustion are a certainty. You may need to find another role. That's how important it is.

But if you manage to secure a clear employer client PSB statement, then each member of the legal team must understand it. This sounds obvious, but many in-house lawyers don't understand business strategy, let alone purpose, and are often embarrassed or, if not, too bloody minded to acknowledge it. Lawyers, due to their training, are not noted for knowing what they don't know, apart from black-letter law. GCs could therefore provide an amnesty for these by hosting workshops in which the basics of business and business strategy are explained to the legal team, ideally by people from the client organisation. Strategy is not complex. It's merely how, in headline terms, a purpose is achieved. But a strategy is not a purpose and it's not a plan. It's how, in headline terms, the organisation will achieve its purpose. The behaviour plan or target operating model is how, over time, the organisation intends to apply its resources, including the legal function, to implement its strategy to achieve its purpose.

3. Step 2: Sell the generic PSB plan of the legal function to the employer client

This is a tricky step, considering that the profession at large has not come up with a clear statement on the role and purpose of in-house lawyers. My advice is to choose your definition, back it up and stick to it. My definition is that the purpose of the legal function within any organisation is to deliver excellent legal counsel and process in the service of that organisation's shared PSB plan, always provided that it makes clear that it has an overriding duty to the court and to society, from which it derives its mandate to practise. My definition doesn't sit well, initially, with many clients; but there are three reasons why this approach can make your life as an in-house lawyer happier:

- It will help you maintain high ethical standards;
- It will buttress your independence; and
- It will give you a solid foundation for budget negotiations.

Whatever your definition of the purpose of the legal function, it is essential that it is clear and shared by everyone in the function; and that it is understood and agreed by the employer client. I acknowledge that this statement is a tall order, but I can trace so many relationship problems that I have encountered in legal functions back to a failure to agree, upfront, the legal function's PSB. I have attended so many in-house conferences at which lawyers say it's time to clarify the role of the in-house function. It never happens. Regulators appear reluctant to offer that clarification. That's no help to the in-house function. You must secure your own. But I find that the subject isn't raised. So, the employer client is left to decide on the role and purpose of the legal function. This doesn't make sense. What profession wants to be told what to do? Did I say to my haematologist, "This is what I want you to do?" What doctor asks a patient what treatment they need? So, tell – don't ask – your employer client what it needs in terms of legal counsel and process to implement its strategy to achieve its purpose. Own, fully, your professional power and asymmetrical knowledge. Don't be bullied. This level of clarity as to your purpose as a practising lawyer is key to feeling fulfilled and being successful at work.

4. Step 3: Set up a legal executive board to run the legal function as a business

Whether your total annual legal spend, including external law firm fees, is in the hundreds of millions or in thousands – it doesn't matter. Legal functions are internal businesses consisting of regulated individuals providing legal services to their employer client. They are internal law firms owned by people who are not lawyers. In the United Kingdom, people who are not lawyers can run law firms under licence – called an alternative business systems (ABS) licence – and run these as businesses. Many of these licences have been issued. Yet the employer clients of in-house legal functions require no licence whatsoever. An anomaly, in my view. They own these internal law firms but don't run them as businesses and frequently don't allow the lawyers to run them as businesses.

Licensed or not, the provision of legal services is a business like any other professional services business and needs to be run as a business. All the art and science of business developed over hundreds of years with well-established, tried-and-tested principles exist because without even one of the main pillars of business efficacy, things go wrong. I find some in-house lawyers at best sceptical of the importance of running the legal function as a business, at worst derisory. I struggle to convince some that they don't know what they don't know about business. For others, whose brightness is central to their identity, conceding that they have something to learn is a concession too far. I have met other lawyers willing to learn. One global GC said that, although initially sceptical, over time their organisation started to see the potential value in the principles I proposed. Another lawyer, who set up a law firm under ABS rules and who followed my advice to structure the law firm as a limited company with a board with a non-executive chair rather than as a partnership, later said it was the best step he had taken. A third – a GC – found the zero-based budgeting approach linked to their employer client's PSB, which I had suggested during their annual budget round, changed the conversation with their CEO.

The most important activity in running any business is decision making. Nothing of lasting value happens without taking thoughtful decisions linked to a shared purpose. An executive board takes the day-to-day decisions of a business. The legal function needs an executive board consisting of five essential discrete functions – finance, marketing, revenue, operations and technology – even if there is only one in-house lawyer who can 'multi-hat' each function. These five functions are usually supported by HR and legal functions. In small organisations, one person can lead more than one of these five functions, provided that each function is given the time it needs. In my business – it's just me – I must cover all five functions and if I let one slip, my business suffers. Here are the headlines for the function leaders required on a legal function's executive board.

The CEO of the legal function is the GC or head of legal. Their purpose, like that of any CEO, is to create an environment in which the legal team thrives; to grow and develop the legal function; and to serve stakeholders – society, the court, their employer client, employees, suppliers and so on. They must come to know the unique needs of each person they lead and try to meet those needs. In this way, the people they lead will feel fulfilled and will be inclined to give much more of their discretionary effort. Growth in a legal department context means ensuring it secures the appropriate budget to hire the appropriate staff levels and resources to deliver on its PSB plan. Securing this people budget depends on the quality of the relationship between the legal function and its employer client so that when it tells – not asks – the organisation what it needs in terms of legal counsel and process, it is believed. A process for negotiating the legal function's needs is set out below. This process will be as successful as the quality of the relationship between the legal function and its employer client. High levels of trust within that relationship are essential.

The next essential cornerstone of the legal operating board is its part-time CFO – a senior qualified accountant borrowed from the finance department or externally sourced. The purpose of this CFO is to take full responsibility for the finances of the legal function; to translate its PSB into a budget; and to sign off on monthly accounts and variance analysis and agree actions to address those variances. I have met GCs who don't know how many lawyers they employ or how to read a profit and loss account. I don't expect them to know; but if they want to build credibility with their employer client, they need to be on top of their finances and only a qualified accountant with strategic finance experience can do that, properly, for them. Not a bookkeeper.

Then the legal operating board needs the equivalent of a COO – who can be a lawyer or not – whose purpose is to convert the legal function's business plan into an operating plan; to create an environment in which that plan can be delivered; and to be responsible for keeping the legal function's promise to the employer client. They know how to get things done. Practice area lawyers can report to this COO.

The legal function also needs technology to enable its strategy and therefore must borrow the equivalent of a CTO from the organisation's IT department or source one externally. Their role is to enable the legal function's strategy using the latest technology; to understand and contribute to the evolving role of technology in law; and to educate and support the legal team in the use of technology. We are not talking about the number of laptops required here, but strategic technology at work. The main problem is that technology professionals, ironically, are often not allowed to do their jobs, are not included in key strategic decisions and are engaged too late on projects in legal functions.

To many, this may feel like an unnecessary luxury, but the legal function's executive board absolutely needs someone – or access to someone – who understands the art and science of marketing and especially internal communications. Frequently in-house lawyers complain to me that their employer client doesn't understand what they do. That's because they don't take responsibility for telling them, properly. They must help to communicate what the function is going do, is doing and has done in order to support the legal function's executive board in presenting its business plan to the organisation and contribute to an ongoing understanding of employer client needs. This could be someone borrowed from the marketing department or externally sourced. It's not about 'comms'. That word demeans the role

People buy people first and in professional services, people are micro-businesses. They must demonstrate, not assert, value.

required. It's about an understanding of classic marketing theory – for example, Kotler's[1] four Ps of product, price, place and promotion. The product is the list of legal services; the price is the function's budget; the place is how, physically, the legal function delivers those services. The final P, promotion, includes internal communication in a legal function context. It's about articulating the legal function's value to the employer client and coordinating monthly storytelling – for example, big wins from litigation, learning from errors made and so-called business as usual activity. It's important that one of the lawyers does not attempt to cover this role. I've tried it with an in-house team and it doesn't work. Professional services expert David Maister[2] observed that marketing is about the demonstration, not the assertion, of competence. So, your legal operating board needs to agree how best to communicate, using expert marketing and communications advice, your value to your employer client. People buy people first and in professional services, people are micro-businesses. They must demonstrate, not assert, value. The payoff for what some considers a luxury will come in each budget round with your employer client.

Finally, your board needs someone to advise on people issues – usually someone from the HR department, or you can source this advice externally. In large organisations, the legal function may have its own chief of staff to support the GC on people issues.

And that's it. Many of these roles can be carried out by one person, but it's important to cover all roles. The benefits are better decisions, better credibility with your employer client and better governance. I find even people on boards who are not lawyers struggle to understand why all five functions must be covered. The reasons why are the same reasons why lawyers don't skip steps in a legal process.

The primary task of your legal executive board is then to draft a three-year business plan, using a zero-based budget starting point and which incorporates a target operating model, congruent with the employer client's PSB plan; to secure sign-off from the employer client on the generic PSB plan of the legal function; and then to sell the draft business plan to the senior leadership team and the board. Sign off on the final draft ensuring it promises only seven things for $7 (see Step 4), and not 10 things for $7. Then secure written protection for the legal function on the three things not paid for by the employer client in the business plan. Empower your legal executive board to deliver its business plan. Finally, deliver only the seven things for which your employer client has paid you to do, and do so excellently; and then constantly communicate up, down and across the organisation what you are doing, have done and are going to do.

The reason why your legal function – no matter how small – should run itself as an internal break-even business run by an executive board is because this is the best structure from which to optimise its relationships. The reason this is an optimal structure is because it maximises trust between with the employer client, with the legal team and with out-of-house advisers.

5. Step 4: Tell – don't ask – your employer client what it needs from your legal function

What does business need from the legal function? This is a frequent topic at legal conferences. Usually, a CEO is wheeled in to answer this question. Why? The answer to me is obvious: the relationship is one of employer-employee first, lawyer second. The extent to which lawyers ask rather than tell their employers what they need varies from lawyer to lawyer. Nevertheless, frequently the culture of the in-house function is to attach its identity to the extent to which it is pleasing its employer. The evidence for this is illustrated in the list of topics at in-house conferences. This culture is good neither for the legal function nor for the employer client. But it is possible, using this model, to reframe the relationship within an employee-employer dynamic. The key step for the legal function is to understand the PSB plan of the organisation in sufficient detail to tell, not ask, the organisation what it needs to achieve its PSB. Then it must cost these needs fully. Let's say your legal function decides your employer client needs 10 things and these cost $10; you can back up this analysis and costing and demonstrate, not assert, the risks to the employer client of dropping any one of the 10 things. If the organisation provides a budget of only $7, then the legal function must do seven things, not 10, and the organisation must understand the risks of not paying for the missing three. If, as I mention several times throughout this book, the legal function does 10 things, it is performing what some in the legal profession describe as a 'diving catch' – a cricket term – to do what has become a dangerous but popular catchphrase in the profession: doing more for less. As if they had been doing less for more all along. Confusing purpose with efficiency hurts everyone.

6. Step 5: Negotiate a legal business plan which meets the organisation's needs but honours the purpose of the legal function

The next step is to sign off on a three-year business plan which meets business needs but honours the purpose of your legal function. By 'business plan', I mean a plan which allows you to run the legal function as a business, not like one. You can use any business plan template. Here are some notes which I hope you find helpful.

6.1 Points to consider in drafting the legal function business plan

Definitions of the following terms should be agreed with your employer client:

- 'legal function';
- 'employer client';
- 'the needs of the employer client';
- 'budget';
- 'legal counsel';
- 'legal process'; and
- 'exclusions' (the list of services that the employer client needs but which cannot be funded within the budget and therefore are not part of the plan).

The purpose of the legal function (P):

- To work with the employer client to foresee risks;
- To provide excellent legal counsel and process; and
- To develop in-house lawyers and lawyer-leaders.

The strategy of the legal function to achieve its purpose (S):

- A strategy statement might look like this: "The primary strategy of the legal function to achieve its purpose will be to focus on communicating how it exploits its employer client's scarce resources to foresee top and emerging risks and to provide essential counsel and process."

The behaviour plan of the legal function to implement its strategy (B):

- Operation as an independent break-even business;
- An emphasis on maximising personal and team performance and fulfilment; and
- Best practice in internal marketing and operational management of scarce resources.

The needs of the employer client:

- Foresight;
- Excellent legal counsel;
- Excellent legal process;
- Value for money; and
- Within budget.

The opportunity to:

- enable better decisions to create a sustainable organisation;
- have a conversation with the business which matches needs to resources;
- create an environment in which people can thrive; and
- protect the environment and society through excellent governance.

Internal marketing plan:

- Internal marketing, not just communications, is a key component of legal strategy. All legal executive board members need to understand what internal marketing is and how it is works in practice. The plan will follow standard marketing principles – that is, the four Ps:
  - Product (service): Foresight: counsel, process.
  - Price: The budget.

- Place (delivery): One to one, one to many, in writing
- Promotion (internal marketing): The in-house function brand: independent; professional, quality; reliable: forward looking, risk managers etc; seminars led by legal team members; relationship marketing – monthly storytelling via email.

Operations plan:
- Business need;
- People;
- Resources;
- IT plan; and
- Finance plan.

People plan:
- Legal function operating board:
  - GC as 'CEO';
  - CFO from finance department or external;
  - COO/practice heads;
  - CTO from IT department or external;
  - CMO from marketing department or external;
  - HR.

  An organisation chart should be attached.

  The legal function executive board will set out, in conjunction with HR, its own people policy, particularly in relation to the creation of a culture of excellence for lawyers and those who support lawyers.
- A separate policy will be agreed by the legal function in respect of external counsel and other providers.

Legal function target operating model:
- Taken together, the sections above constitute the legal function's target operating model, which is about how, ideally, the legal function would like to operate. The components of the target operating model are needs, strategic resources and strategic processes:
  - Needs: The agreed needs of the business.

- Strategic resources: People, external relationships, knowledge.
- Strategic processes: Operating board, external advisers, workflows.

Finance:
- Detailed budget;
- Financial reporting processes; and
- Monthly management accounting reports with variance analysis and narrative to be presented to the legal function executive board.

SWOT and mitigation:
- Strengths;
- Weaknesses;
- Opportunities;
- Threats; and
- Mitigation.

Business plan steps:
- Debate and agree Draft 1 at legal executive board meetings.
- Sell Draft 1 to the employer client (see selling techniques in earlier chapters).
- Debate.
- Review and agree Draft 2 at the legal executive board meeting.
- Re-present Draft 2 to the business.
- Repeat as required, sign off and deliver.

7. Step 6: Reframe your relationship with external advisers

What if your external legal services providers could support your legal function in reframing its relationship with your employer client by helping it reframe how key issues are viewed? Here is a typical list of key issue headings:
- **Efficiency:** The legal function and its employer client should agree on what the word 'efficiency' means before attempting to improve it. External advisers could help.
- **Risk:** Some employer clients view anticipating and mitigating

legal risk as the responsibility of the legal function alone, whereas it can reasonably be viewed as a joint responsibility. This is an argument process that external advisers should support.

- **Controlling costs:** The legal function may fail to communicate value for money because they are not trained in internal value-for-money communications. They can become targets as poor cost controllers. External advisers could be particularly helpful on this subject.
- **Reducing costs:** The legal function may fail to connect its spend to strategic outcomes and allow itself to be boxed into a corner on 'doing more for less' when sometimes it needs to spend more, not less, to achieve those outcomes. For example, the legal function and its employer client can agree on reducing contracting costs; but how does it sell-in a case for spending more money on conduct risk, defined as behaviour by executives over time? External advisers could help with making this case.
- **Delivery:** This is the area which has advanced the most in recent years, but even delivery can be frustrated if the role and purpose of the legal function in the organisation are not clear and shared. External advisers could be part of finding a solution to this problem and not seen as part the problem.
- **Dashboards:** Legal function data dashboards have improved in recent years, but the ability of the legal function to make informed decisions based on data varies considerably depending on the alignment between business purpose and the legal function's purpose. External advisers with expertise in strategic data analysis can help with this issue.
- **Collaboration:** Successful cross-functional collaboration depends on high EQ skills. These vary considerably among in-house lawyers and out-of-house advisers. Advisers need to acknowledge the importance of EQ for mutual benefit.

So, what if your external legal services providers were able to join with your legal function to help tease out these issues rather than responding to instructions? What if you asked them to take a consultative approach? EY Law's 2021 Survey states that:

If there is no 'one size fits all' route, it follows that if your external legal services provider could help you overcome your issues, then why not involve them?

... General Counsel are aware of ... challenges with only 52% reporting that their department's day-to-day work is aligned with the broader business strategy ... 30% are considering creating a co-sourcing or outsourcing relationship with a third-party provider to manage parts of the legal function. This alone demonstrates that there is no one-size-fits-all route to transformation.[3]

If there is no 'one size fits all' route, it follows that if your external legal services provider could help you overcome your issues, then why not involve them? The full range of your external provider's specific capabilities should be called into service on this journey. In addition, to bring about change, your provider will need to incubate critical missing capabilities to engage with your legal function on a bespoke basis on your personal leadership PSB in respect of running the legal function as a break-even internal business; and to develop the confidence to tell, not ask, the employer client what it needs in terms of excellent legal counsel and process to achieve its strategic objectives.

Often, legal functions won't let external providers near their senior leadership team. They fear being circumvented. Equally, external providers often don't or won't help legal functions fix their relationship with their employer clients. Meanwhile, the employer client is unaware of the nuances of these relationships, resulting in greater risks. Apart from in-house conference organisers asking token CEOs to tell them "What the business needs from legal", in-house and out-of-house lawyers never get together in any meaningful way and in large numbers with employer clients at conferences.

8. Step 7: Ensure the GC acts as the CEO of the legal function

The final step in reframing the relationship between the in-house legal function and its employer client is for in-house lawyers to defy their law school training when it comes to leadership processes. Law schools don't value leadership because law firms don't value it, because they can't bill it by the hour and because legal training eschews feelings. In-house lawyers must accept that one of their number – the GC – is the CEO of the legal function and must lead, and they must submit to that leadership. It's an action, not a thought. All leaders do three things and so must lawyers-as-leaders:

- **Create an environment in which the people they lead thrive:** Some lawyers-as-leaders struggle with this. They are often litigators trained not only to win, but also to ensure that the other side loses. The notion that they might *help someone else win* does not compute. It's counterintuitive. That's why GCs must pay more attention than they think to leadership development – their own, particularly.
- **Grow and develop the function they lead:** GCs must grow and develop the legal function as a business because they are spending someone else's money.
- **Serve stakeholders – all of them, not just some:** These include the court, society, the employer client represented by its board, employees and suppliers. People died in trenches to allow lawyers to practise in a democracy. Society expects lawyers to bear society in mind when advising their employer clients. This expectation will intensify as businesses realise that ESG decision making is here to stay. It's not a fad. Regulators are slowly waking up to this reality.

GCs and lawyers-as-leaders might consider taking the advice of Warren Buffet's associate Charlie Munger: "Never, ever think about something else when you should be thinking about the power of incentives."[4] He was not just referring to financial incentives. Lawyers-as-leaders need to consider soft incentives for those they lead. Leading is a verb – an action. Lawyers who lead must lead.

Finally, a good friend of mine, Loughlin Hickey, suggested that I end this book by inviting you to reflect on what is holding you back. What do you fear if people see a change in you? What burden could be lifted; what joy experienced if you changed? He says that it's in moments of reflection that the wonder happens, the possibilities emerge and the joy of change overshadows the fear. He's right. I hope this book brings you more peace, and even joy, in your life and work *Most Mondays*.[5]

Cancer has taught me that the pursuit of peace and joy within, and those you love without, is all that matters.

Notes

1   Philip Kotler, *Marketing Insights from A to Z: 80 Concepts Every Manager Needs to Know*, John Wiley & Sons, 2003.
2   David H Maister, *Managing the Professional Service Firm*, Simon & Schuster, 2003.
3   Cornelius Grossmann, "The General Counsel Imperative: How do you turn barriers into building blocks?", EY, 7 April 2021, www.ey.com/en_uk/law/general-counsel-imperative-barriers-building-blocks#:~:text=General%20Counsel%20are%20aware%20of,adding%20value%20to%20the%20business.
4   Charles T Munger, "The Psychology of Human Misjudgement", speech transcript available at: https://jamesclear.com/great-speeches/psychology-of-human-misjudgment-by-charlie-munger.
5   The title of my next book.

Appendix 1: Inherent tension in-house: defusing the law department time bomb at a time of pandemic[1]

Ciarán Fenton

There is, according to the evidence, a correlation between serious corporate risk events which affect society and the inherent tension in the relationship between in-house lawyers, required to serve the regulatory societal objectives of the 2007 Legal Services Act, and their business employers who pay and direct them. Is this a systemic weakness? Does it constitute a significant risk time bomb for society? Will the corporate stress caused by the pandemic exacerbate the inherent tension? The purpose of this article is to explore these risks and to suggest ways of mitigating them.

Introduction

I stumbled into the world of in-house lawyers (IHLs) many years ago when, as a leadership consultant, I helped a general counsel to find a new role as a lawyer-leader, as I like to call them. It was his last role, and he was looking ahead to his post-corporate portfolio career. He asked me to research legal education, an area he was interested in pursuing. He felt that lawyers were underprepared for business life. That piece of research led me to a world of which I was unaware, to people I would otherwise never have met and, ultimately, to work engagements with hundreds of lawyers, teams and boards in-house and out, across the world as well as unanticipated speaking and writing opportunities. This is one of those writing opportunities. I was not new to the legal world. I majored in law in my business degree and in my corporate career, I spent much of my time working on deals with lawyers. I also ran divisional businesses for large organisations and have extensive experience as a non-lawyer (sic) working with CEOs, CXOs, NEDs, boards and teams.

Legal Services Act 2007

Of the eight regulatory objectives defined in the Legal Services Act 2007,[2] from which in-house lawyers derive their authority, the first of these – public interest – is the focus of this article. IHLs have a long track record of preventative counselling which protects the business and society. Those practising in heavily regulated industries like drugs, food and banking have a tougher role than unregulated sectors. Even in non-regulated businesses, there are requirements that mitigate risks, all of which IHLs track. Their hard work and successes are frequently undercelebrated, underfunded and underappreciated partly because they provide credence services[3] and partly because they are neither trained in the art and science of internal communications nor see value in hiring those that are. The problem is not what IHLs are doing well or that most are highly ethical – these points are not controversial – it's whether or not, over time, the inherent tension in the relationship between IHLs and their employers has adversely impacted the public interest regulatory objective of the 2007 Act to such an extent that it's only a matter of time before a front-page risk event implicating IHLs directly occurs and of such magnitude that the public and their public representatives clamour for something to be done about IHLs thereby catching modern legal practice on the back foot, as it were. Does the evidence support the existence of this time bomb and is it more likely to explode in the context of a pandemic, at which time the inherent tension[4] may be exacerbated?

Leveson and other stories

Ask a lawyer to cite a case involving an in-house lawyer, and they will invariably refer to the *Brett* case which emerged from the Leveson Inquiry in 2011.

The Leveson Inquiry was a judicial public inquiry into the culture, practices and ethics of the British press following the News International phone-hacking scandal, chaired by Lord Justice Leveson, who was appointed in July 2011.

Alastair Brett was formerly legal manager at Times Newspapers Ltd. The Leveson inquiry considered Mr Brett's actions in connection with a 2009 story in *The Times* which revealed the author of an anonymous blog entitled 'Nightjack', chronicling the life of a police officer.

The following exchange took place at the hearing:

> *Mr Alastair Brett*
> *If I'm approached by somebody for legal advice, and I was, I think I would regard that as covered by legal professional privilege.*
>
> *Lord Justice Leveson*
> *I'll have to think about that.*
>
> *Mr Alastair Brett*
> *It raises all sorts of interesting questions about in-house lawyers.*
>
> *Lord Justice Leveson*
> *Indeed.*[5]

In analysing the implications of these exchanges and the outcome of the Inquiry and subsequent Solicitor's Disciplinary Tribunal, Richard Moorhead, Steven Vaughan and Cristina Godinho observe in *In-House Lawyers' Ethics*:

> *If we look at in-house conduct in terms of risk, the decision not to*

impose some form of entity regulation on legal teams does not make much sense either. Weigh the harms caused by SCB's wire-stripping, or Rolls-Royce's corruption, against the more standard fare of SRA enforcement (solicitors taking client money, misleading the court), and we are hard pushed to see that in-house practice is low risk.[6]

Successive governments did not introduce any form of entity regulation on legal teams in the United Kingdom after the *Brett* case or indeed after the many scandals involving in-house lawyers some of which are set out in the introduction to *In-House Lawyers' Ethics* (pp3–4) and, in respect of which the list according to the authors, "suggests that the in-house role is an ethically compromised endeavour". Their list includes:

- General Motors: ignition-switch scandal;
- Enron: accounting transactions issue;
- Arthur Andersen: document retention policies;
- Apple: stock options backdating;
- Energy Solutions: employee witness bonuses;
- Siemens: business consulting agreements;
- government examples include advice given in the United States and the United Kingdom on Iraq War matters.

Do the *Brett* case and this list merely prove that some IHLs struggle with the inherent tension or are they symptomatic of a deeper malaise within the structure of law departments? The UCL Moral Compass Report 2016 helps us answer this question, at least in part.

The Moral Compass Report

The *Mapping the Moral Compass*[7] report was published by the UCL Centre for Ethics and Law as part of its Ethical Leadership for In-House Lawyers Initiative in 2016. The headline findings included:

- 10–15% (of the in-house lawyers surveyed) experienced elevated ethical pressure;
- 30–40% sometimes experienced ethical pressure;
- 36% agreed that loopholes in the law should be identified that benefit the business;

- 9% indicated saying "no" to the organisation was to be avoided, even when there is no legally acceptable alternative to suggest;
- 65% reported that achieving what their organisation wants has to be their main priority; and
- 7% never discussed professional ethics issues with colleagues internally or externally, formally or informally.

The authors of the survey found that there were four categories of in-house lawyer:
- the capitulators;
- the coasters;
- the comfortably numb; and
- the champions.

The report had a mixed reaction. Rhymer Rigby wrote in the *Financial Times* at the time of publication:

> *A recent piece of research from University College London on in-house lawyers, Mapping the Moral Compass, has caused a stir in the legal community. It identifies four main ethical groups of in-house lawyers: the capitulators, the coasters, the comfortably numb and the champions. Perhaps unsurprisingly, some general counsel have taken exception to these characterisations.*[8]

Unsurprising indeed. GCs assume that their integrity is being impugned when challenged on the moral compass issue. Seeing the problem through their lens, they feel understandably outraged at the suggestion that, as one GC put it, all IHLs leave "their morality at the door when going in-house". But no one is suggesting all do, but that some do and indeed did, according to the evidence. While different personality types manage morality differently, as the percentages in the Moral Compass survey demonstrate, GCs cannot deny (and don't to me) that many decide or are convinced by the business environment in which they operate that they must dilute or play down their status as regulated professional officers of the court to a greater or lesser extent. How often do we hear lawyers at in-house conferences insist that "I'm a business person first, lawyer second"?

Why else has the term 'in-house' sustained? No other function in business is defined in terms of its relationship with out of house. In-house CFOs don't exist. Law firms have no incentive, therefore, at present, to rock the boat.

The first time I heard a GC use that phrase was at an in-house conference; within months that GC's organisation was at the centre of a front-page corporate scandal. I suspect that, at that moment, no one cared how good a business person they were but how good a lawyer they were in helping their client – the organisation – survive the crisis. I also suspect that that organisation was quick to take advantage of privileged conversations with that GC, a privilege granted by society, not to all function heads in the business.

If you Google the words "business-person-first-lawyer-second" most of the initial hits are from law firms. They have no current incentive to encourage GCs to be "lawyers first and business people second" because that would risk cutting the umbilical cord that connects law firms to GCs: most GCs come from law firms; are protected by them in tough times; and the cord helps maintain the fiction that solicitors in and out of house are the same. Why else has the term 'in-house' sustained? No other function in business is defined in terms of its relationship with out of house. In-house CFOs don't exist. Law firms have no incentive, therefore, at present, to rock the boat. Hence their muted response to Section 4.12 of the Independent Review of Legal Services Regulation (IRLSR). By muted I mean, in some cases, no response at all, and from a legal services business perspective, who would blame them? Perhaps this reflects the fragility of their business model. One GC said to me: "... outside counsel tend to be more conservative in their opinions than in-house lawyers because they have to be or risk being sued." Equally, IHLs risk being bullied if they are too conservative, according to the evidence. Society doesn't get a look in.

Section 4.12 of the IRLSR

The Centre for Ethics and Law, University College London, published a report on 11 June 2020 written by Professor Stephen Mayson with the title "Reforming Legal Services – Regulation Beyond the Echo Chambers – Final Report of the Independent Review of Legal Services Regulation".[9]

Section 4.12 relates to "Corporate legal departments and in-house lawyers" and in respect of which Professor Mayson makes a recommendation, Recommendation 20, as follows:

> *An in-house legal department should be capable, for regulatory purposes, of being registered as a distinct business unit, so that the department's delivery of legal services would be subject to the same regulatory obligations as any other registered provider. Individuals within such a registered in-house unit should also be registered personally if they carry on activities for which before-the-event authorisation or personal accreditation would otherwise be required.*

Professor Mayson sets out his reasons for this recommendation as follows:

> *There is little doubt that a tension is inherent in this relationship when the client for legal services is also the adviser's employer. The usual expectation of 'independent' legal advice is often stretched ... [It is] arguable that those with professional obligations might benefit from further regulatory support ... In principle, they should not be at risk of dismissal or disadvantage simply for observing their professional obligations ... This might entail express conditions in their employment contract, and a direct reporting line to the Board ... As we have seen in recent years, corporate failures can lead to consumer and societal detriment. In-house lawyers have to be able to sound alarm bells without the chilling effect of potential reprisal.*

The words "chilling effect of potential reprisal" are indeed chilling when you consider the impact of corporate failures on society and which failures, more often than not, hit the more vulnerable parts of society.

So why did Section 4.12 not receive more attention from lawyers, business and regulators given the gravity of its conclusion in terms of societal risk? I guess that most IHLs don't see the problem as a problem of their making or one which they can solve and also because their solo training doesn't encourage them to think in those terms. Law firms have no incentive to comment as set out above. Businesses – based on my work mediating between the legal function and the employer client business – are unaware of the time bomb, would struggle with GCs not reporting to CEOs, and just don't get the risk; regulators, understandably from their perspective, don't want to take on the poisoned chalice of fixing a problem that successive governments have failed to identify let alone address. They may argue that successive governments have ignored the societal objectives of Section 1 of the 2007 Legal Services Act as is the case with the spirit of Section 172 of the Companies Act which is also often ignored. Who wants to take on big business?

Time of pandemic

But if organisations care only for their business' profitability in the short term, they will find that COVID-19 has created an environment in which they will be out of step with the public mood especially if they took advantage of COVID-19 public financing. Society will expect in-house lawyers to get in step with this mood or else lawyers may find society will take legal services regulation out of their hands and in a manner which may make the second state of affairs worse than the first.

Meanwhile many in-house lawyers see the writing on the wall but are not sure what to do about it in the short term. Below I set out seven steps they might consider. But first, they may wish to reflect on three current trends which may incentivise them to take action:

- The environment, society and governance (ESG) movement is here to stay. Lawyers in-house and out will be required by their clients to support ESG and to enable the relaunch of capitalism[10] especially in the light of COVID-19 financing to high-profile companies – see list.[11]
- The poor mental health and wellbeing of lawyers[12] are receiving more considered attention and, in the light of the success of the #MeToo movement, there is a trend towards confronting the status quo. A growing minority of lawyers are starting to, counter-intuitively, have each other's backs. Were a number of these to break ranks, ignore their NDAs and come out – that would be, as some characterise it, a game-changer.

As one GC put it to me: "Bluntly, there needs to be greater leadership from the very best in-house legal leaders/influencers, and ultimately government regulation which effectively codifies the purpose of an in-house team."

- The business model of legal services is coming under increasing scrutiny as consumers – retail and business – are waking up to its flaws.

When I confront lawyers – in-house and out – with the risks, their counter-arguments include:

- I don't see the problem. My boss is great, and I don't encounter major ethical issues.
- Ethics are not the sole responsibility of lawyers. That's the role of compliance.
- Who's to say a significant risk event can be traced to IHLs? There are lots of factors.

Surprisingly, none is willing to address the specific charge that IHLs are to a greater or lesser extent dependent on their employers and therefore cannot always act independently as required by the regulator, nor is there a consensus on the specific points of the IRLSR Report Section 4.12. Surprising because one would have expected lawyers to be swayed by evidence and they're not. I can only assume that they feel it's a problem not of their making and one they feel they cannot fix.

I disagree with this assessment. It is of their making since few would doubt that Section 4.12 of the Mayson Report would become law tomorrow if enough high-profile lawyers in-house and out lobbied for it. As one GC put it to me: "Bluntly, there needs to be greater leadership from the very best in-house legal leaders/influencers, and ultimately government regulation which effectively codifies the purpose of an in-house team." They don't because they, as yet, see no incentive in doing do. The public interest argument does not move them because they don't see law-making as their role or responsibility and law firms, on which IHLs rely heavily, fear what might happen to their substantial commercial fee income if the status quo were to be challenged.

In respect of regulation, one GC said:

Regulators, I suspect, rather than seeing the risk and not wanting to address it, simply haven't yet clocked the link between public interest and corporate failure. They see consumers as the biggest area of risk and focus there. In house lawyers can look after themselves and resign if needed – no big deal.

I find this puzzling – if the regulator doesn't see the link it means it is wilfully ignoring the first regulatory objective of the 2007 Act. Why would it do that unless it doesn't believe that society is serious about taking on poor business behaviour and therefore ignores that objective? Another GC quipped: "If we can't get people to address climate change, what chance legal supervision!"

But self-interest may incentivise IHLs to take at least some steps to mitigate the risks they face in what none refute is a rapidly changing environment. Over the last five years, I have piloted a seven-step in-house target operating model (in-house TOM) in several organisations in the United Kingdom and in the United States. My intention is that these might become the framework for self-regulation – a sort of 'Mayson S4.12 Pilot'.

A seven-step in-house TOM to help defuse the time bomb

- **Step 1 – Agree a shared language on the current purpose, strategy and behaviour (PSB) of the business.** One GC told me that many lawyers don't know how to contribute to the broader strategic planning process and therefore don't spend time on it, in which case they should have the humility to ask, just as the business should ask them about the legal process.
- **Step 2 – Decide, don't ask, what the business needs from Legal.** Decide, within the law department and with advice from outside it, what the business needs in terms of legal counsel and process to achieve its PSB plan. The business doesn't know what it needs. If it did, it wouldn't need lawyers. Lawyers do know or at least should know.
- **Step 3 – Set up a Legal Operating Board to run Legal as a business, not like one.** Set up a Legal Operating Board consisting of lawyers and non-lawyers (sic) from Finance, IT and Internal Communications to run Legal as an internal breakeven business. All the art and science of business applies

to Legal. Conversely, if Legal does not apply well-established business principles it will struggle to convince the business that it can deliver the essential 'ten things for ten dollars'.

- **Step 4 – Take responsibility for selling the purpose of Legal to your board.** I hear from GCs that the business is not interested in Legal until there's a problem. Therefore, they must sell the purpose of Legal to their board, even before they present their Legal Business Plan. The generic purpose (P) of any legal department is to enable better decisions by their board in terms of legal counsel and process that benefit the business and society under the objectives set out in the 2007 Act from which law departments derive their authority. The generic strategy (S) of any legal department should be to act as an independent internal business. The generic behaviour (B) of any legal department should be to deliver 'ten things for ten dollars' excellently or seven for seven, but never ten for seven.
- **Step 5 – Invest in innovative law firms.** Invest in long-term relationships with innovative law firms, allowing them access to the C-suite so that they can help close the gap with Legal. The problem is, as one equity partner explained to me: "... we advise businesses how to get from A to B. This involves counsel and process. We undercharge for counsel and overcharge for process. But it nets out ok in the end ...". It may "net out ok" for some law firms, but society is underserved, and soon it will clamour for change.
- **Step 6 – Negotiate a business plan which meets business needs but honours Legal's purpose.** By 'negotiate' I mean to negotiate a deal with the board where Legal agrees to deliver 'seven things for seven dollars not ten things for seven dollars'. This requires selling skills and negotiating skills, ensuring the business feels that this approach is in its long-term interests. By 'business plan' I mean a plan which allows you to run Legal as a business, not like one, over the next three to five years.
- **Step 7 – Accept that the GC is the CEO of Legal.** The final step is for in-house lawyers to defy their law school training when it comes to leadership. Law schools don't value leadership because law firms can't bill leadership by the hour. In-house

> lawyers must accept that one of their number – the GC – is the CEO of Legal who must value the purpose of lawyers as leaders:
> - to create an environment in which the people in the law department thrive;
> - to develop the legal department in every respect; and
> - to serve all stakeholders: people, the business and society.

These are actions, not intellectual endeavours nor, as one lawyer suggested to me, "Socratic processes". One GC said to me that my suggestion of running legal as a business is "too simplistic". I disagree. These principles are simple, not simplistic, and while the journey is not without challenges, can IHLs afford to do nothing? Another GC answers this question:

Unfortunately for many, that statement will elicit the answer 'yes, I can afford to do nothing'. As such 'failing conventionally' doesn't look like too bad an option, especially if it is slowly, rather than risk doing something and being wrong.

If that GC is correct and I am wrong, then the status quo will survive. But if I am right and there are several front-page risk events directly linked to IHLs and society demands, as part of the ESG movement emboldened by the pandemic, that the societal first objective of the 2007 Act is observed, then the time bomb will explode under IHLs and modern legal practice, as it stands, will not be prepared. If I were an IHL at the start or middle of my career, I'd care about that risk.

Notes

1   First published in *Modern Lawyer*, published by Globe Law and Business, October 2020. For further information visit: www.globelawandbusiness.com/journals/Modern-Lawyer-Journal.
2   Section 1, Legal Services Act 2007.
3   Francisco Cabrillio and Sean Fitzpatrick, *The Economics of Courts and Litigation*, Edward Elgar, 2008, p159.
4   Stephen Mayson, *Independent Review of Legal Services Regulation* (UCL, 2020), Section 4.12.
5   https://leveson.sayit.mysociety.org/hearing-15-march-2012/mr-alastair-brett#s55267.
6   Richard Moorhead, Steven Vaughan and Cristina Godinho, *In-House Lawyers' Ethics: Institutional Logics, Legal Risk and the Tournament of Influence* (Hart Publishing, 2019), p228.
7   Richard Moorhead, Cristina Godinho, Steven Vaughan, Paul Gilbert and Stephen Mayson, *Mapping the Moral Compass: The Relationships between In-House Lawyers' Role, Professional Orientations, Team Cultures, Organisational Pressures, Ethical Infrastructure and Ethical Inclination* (2 June 2016), https://ssrn.com/abstract=2784758 or http://dx.doi.org/10.2139/ssrn.2784758.
8   Rhymer Rigby, "In-house legal teams balance profit against morality", *Financial Times*, 21 June 2016, www.ft.com/content/c264c0d2-234e-11e6-9d4d-c11776a5124d.
9   Stephen Mayson, *Reforming Legal Services – Regulation Beyond the Echo Chambers – Final Report of the Independent Review of Legal Services Regulation*, The Centre for Ethics and Law, University College London, June 2020, www.ucl.ac.uk/ethics-law/sites/ethics-law/files/irlsr_final_report_final_0.pdf.

10   www.ft.com/content/957a6514-66c4-11ea-800d-da70cff6e4d3.
11   www.bankofengland.co.uk/news/2020/may/update-to-the-covid-corporate-financing-facility.
12   www.lawgazette.co.uk/law/profession-facing-talent-drain-as-mental-health-problems-surge/5065836.article.

Appendix 2: Lawyers and their regulators can make or break the ESG movement[1]

Ciarán Fenton

There are many perspectives on ESG but few doubt it is here to stay. Inevitably lawyers in-house and out will play a big part in its implementation. This article sets out to explore how lawyers and regulators could make or, perhaps, break it.

The ESG (environmental, social and governance) movement is enjoying mixed success. Its supporters point to the trillions of dollars invested in impact funds, while its detractors say it's all deeply shallow PR. Nevertheless, the direction of travel is clear: ESG is here to stay. The reasons depend on your perspective.

Sara Bernow, who leads McKinsey's work in sustainable investing and co-leads their institutional investing practice in Europe, illustrates one perspective – the business case – in a May 2020 podcast:

We looked at the reasons behind the relationship between ESG performance and financial outcomes and identified five sources of fundamental business value that explain these findings. The first is top-line growth. If you are a consumer goods company with a stronger sustainability proposition, you are more likely to attract customer loyalty and new customer segments. There is evidence that brands with more sustainable impact grow faster than brands that have a less sustainable proposition. On the business-to-business side, there also is a link. Large companies are seeking to channel ESG through their value chain. If you want to be a supplier to one of the world's largest retailers, for example, you had better have a strong sustainability proposition on plastics, packaging, water use, and so on. The second aspect is cost. If you are more resource-efficient, more water-efficient, have less packaging, you will generally have a lower unit-cost structure. The third area are your regulatory relationships. If you are more responsible about your assets' environmental footprint, then the chances of an adverse, punitive regulatory outcome are lower, so there is potentially regulatory value here. The fourth is talent. These days, newer recruits and millennials demand purposeful work and if you are an employer that can meet that need, you will attract and retain that talent, and likely have higher productivity in the workplace. The evidence suggests that this is worth roughly 2 percent of your stock price each year. Then the fifth factor we found is investment optimisation. There are downside risks of holding assets that become stranded. Coal assets and oil tankers, for example, have seen significant write-downs in recent years. Conversely, there are enormous opportunities in ESG-related investments. For example, there is a huge demand for technology that could improve air quality. When you add up all five factors, they explain this roughly 10 percent advantage in your cost of capital.

Simon French, chief economist at Panmure Gordon, illustrates a more nuanced perspective as set out in his piece for London's *Evening Standard* in September 2021, which views measurement and reporting as open to "selective interpretation" by company management teams:

On the environment side, this has led to accusation of "greenwashing" – a situation where a company reports on the environmental measures that present it in the most favourable light. Similar criticisms are faced by businesses that commit to particularly salient social issues and are selective about their governance standards. This is where ESG and sustainable investing needs to be allowed to transition from a blunt "invest or divest" approach to something with more nuance.

The Financial Reporting Council (FRC) illustrates a third perspective – a regulatory one – in their decision in September 2021 to exclude one-third of the 189 applicants, including Schroders, Morgan Stanley Investment Management and Rothschild Wealth Management, from their list of successful signatories to the revised UK code, which sets standards for asset managers, pension schemes and insurers to explain how they are creating "long-term value for clients and beneficiaries leading to sustainable benefits for the economy". For the first time, applicants were required to show detailed evidence of how their actions complied. (*Evening Standard*, 6 September 2021)

My perspective is that the words 'environment', 'society' and 'governance' have a clear meaning and, in combination, are here to stay. The search for metrics for ESG reporting will eventually deliver acceptable if imperfect codes because society – the S in ESG – is skilled at designing workable regulations when it must. It must do so, not least because businesses drew down substantial sums of taxpayers' money during the pandemic, and society will hold them to a much higher standard of behaviour than previously. ESG is becoming the shorthand for that standard. A new term – 'climate change' – has replaced 'global warming' and has caught the public imagination. The press and politicians ask questions about business behaviour regarding the environment, and companies feel that heat. The MeToo and D, E&I movements – all part of the S – are in full voice, forcing companies to respond. Fresh corporate scandals (The Post Office Limited and RICS, to mention just two) are keeping governance – the G – in the headlines.

But what's to stop ESG from going the way of CSR, which enjoyed a similar fillip after the Global Financial Crash in 2008 before losing momentum later? Or put another way, who could do what to ensure that ESG doesn't stall?

In-house lawyers can enable better ESG-based decisions by their boards. Their out-of-house law firm advisers can help them do so.

Lawyers and their regulators are in a strong position – placed as they are at the intersection of law, compliance and governance – to make or break the ESG movement. In-house lawyers (IHLs) can enable better ESG-based decisions by their boards. Their out-of-house law firm advisers can help them do so.

The opposite will happen if IHLs don't engage fully with ESG or if their bosses won't allow them to do so and/or if their law firm advisers talk the ESG talk but don't walk the walk themselves. Law firms are keen to remind GCs how core they are to ESG implementation:

> As companies increase their commitment to sustainability and responsible business, so too has the involvement of the legal team. General counsel and in-house legal teams (and their external advisers) have always played an important role in managing social, ethical and environmental issues for organisations. However, legal teams are no longer just reacting to ESG issues, but proactively becoming involved in integrating material ESG risks and opportunities in business organisations, their operational policies and go-to-market strategies. The following key themes are emerging … (DLA Piper – website 3 December 2020).

> Is ESG the opportunity GCs have been waiting for? With global ESG assets at more than $30tn and expected to grow further, ESG will help define the future for business and society. General Counsel (GCs) have a powerful opportunity to steer businesses towards sustainability and Timothy Wilkins, Global Partner for Client Sustainability, recently led a discussion to investigate how lawyers will play a central role. He was joined by Kirin Kalsi, Head of Legal UK for E-ON; Keith Carr, General Counsel at Lafarge Holcim; and Chris Allen, General Counsel for Corporate, Commercial and Institutional Banking and General Counsel for Europe and America at Standard Chartered Bank. Kicking off the webinar, Wilkins noted that sustainability and the economic, social and governance aspects of ESG have all now moved into the core of board strategy and C-suite decision making … (Freshfields – Blog 7 June 2021).

How are top law firms advising clients in the hot ESG practice area? Reuters Legal wanted to find out, so we put together a panel of sustainability experts who created a fictitious tractor company facing environmental, social and governance issues. We asked law firms to give fictitious Brighton Tractor Supply Co advice that takes advantage of ESG lawyers' creativity and ingenuity in this growing legal field. Here are the 18 law firms that responded: Baker Botts; Ballard Spahr; Crowell & Moring; Fox Rothschild; Hogan Lovells; K&L Gates; King & Spalding; Kirkland & Ellis; Mayer Brown; McDermott Will & Emery; Mintz, Levin, Cohn, Ferris, Glovsky and Popeo; Orrick Herrington & Sutcliffe; Paul Hastings; Pillsbury Winthrop Shaw Pittman; Ropes & Gray; Schiff Hardin; Stroock & Stroock & Lavan; and Troutman Pepper Hamilton Sanders. (Reuters – Scenario Test 28 July 2021.*

Issues around ESG have increasingly become a vital focus within the financial services industry and dominated conversations at board meetings. Legal teams within businesses and organisations can play a much bigger role driving the ESG strategy instead of being an implementer of the regulations and business strategies. That's the key message from a roundtable co-hosted by The Lawyer and Irwin Mitchell's chief commercial officer Victoria Brackett, where a delegation of senior in-house legal counsel shared their thoughts on the progress made so far, practical advice and experience in dealing with challenging situations. "ESG is going to sit at the centre of all our strategies and purpose moving forward," said Brackett. "There's been an acceleration moving from tick box exercises, and lawyers can become advocates of ESG at board level and make sure key messages are heard ... It is critical for in-house lawyers to go beyond being the guardians of compliance and take on a wider role around ethically driving ESG through the strategy in the business. But getting the right structure and the right business culture balance is essential." (The Lawyer roundtable: How legal teams can use ESG to drive purposeful change – 2 August 2021).

So, we can assume:
- ESG is here to stay;
- GCs can play a big part in it; and
- law firms are, unsurprisingly, keen that they do.

What can go wrong?
- Law firms' ESG practices fail because their firms fail to practise ESG;
- GCs fail to lead holistically on ESG, cleaving only to the regulatory aspects; and
- The SRA fails to support GCs in acting with independence in respect of ESG advice to their employers.

Law firms have a woeful track record in the S and G of ESG:

Women still missing from top ranks of law firms: According to an extensive data project conducted by the Financial Times, women are still sorely under-represented at the highest echelons of the industry. Data collected from the largest UK and US firms in London, using a list derived from The Lawyer magazine's rankings, revealed a sharp drop-off in the number of women as they progress up the legal ranks, compounded by stark pay gaps between the sexes, particularly at higher levels. The £28bn legal profession is one of Britain's most important exports but, like other financial and professional services sectors, remains among the most male-dominated industries globally. The FT's research shows that while there are now more women practising law in the UK than men, and just under half of associates – mid-ranking lawyers – in the firms sampled were women, only about a fifth of senior lawyers – or partners – were female. Most firms only increased the proportion of women in their partnerships by a percentage point or less year on year. (Financial Times – 2 January 2020).

Research shows that one in 15 junior lawyers has had suicidal thoughts. The issue of stress among junior lawyers returns to the spotlight this week, with research showing that the proportion claiming to have recently experienced mental ill-health has risen sharply over the past year – and that 6.4% have experienced suicidal thoughts. These are among the findings of the third Junior Lawyers Division resilience and wellbeing survey, published at the weekend. Of more than 1,800 respondents, 48% said they had experienced mental ill-health in the last month, up from 38% last year (an increase of 26%).

Some 93.5% of respondents said they experienced stress in their role. A quarter of those experienced 'severe/extreme' levels of stress. The most frequently mentioned consequences of work-related stress were disrupted sleep (66%) and a negative impact on mental health, including anxiety, emotional upset, fatigue, and negative and depressed thoughts (60%). Meanwhile, 6.4% of respondents (amounting to more than 100 junior lawyers) said they had experienced suicidal thoughts. (*The Law Society Gazette* – 8 April 2019).

Finally, little has changed in the governance (G) of law firms since Laura Empson wrote this piece in 2015:

> *Leaders, by definition, must have followers. In most studies of leadership, this statement is self-evident. Such studies assume that hierarchical relationships within organisations are relatively stable, and take for granted that the most senior people in an organisation have the formal authority to lead it. In law firms, however, the distinction between leaders and followers is more difficult, as traditional hierarchies are replaced by more ambiguous and negotiated relationships among professional peers. As the client relationship partner in one global law firm expressed this to me:*
>
> *Empson: Does anyone have power over you?*
>
> *Partner: Not as far as I'm concerned, no.*
>
> *Empson: Does anyone think they have power over you?*
>
> *Partner: I don't think so.*
>
> *In recent years, I have undertaken two major UK government-funded*

research studies into governance and leadership in global professional service firms. Through these studies I have conducted more than 400 interviews in almost 20 countries with leaders and partners from many of the world's leading professional service firms. These interviews have been supplemented by archival and observational analysis. With regard to the legal sector, through my research and consulting I have worked closely with 15 of the world's leading law firms in the United Kingdom, Europe and the United States. I have found that in law firms, which are filled with highly educated, independent thinkers, who do not like being told what to do, it is not easy to find lawyers who are happy to identify themselves as followers. Furthermore, finding lawyers who are happy to put themselves forward as leaders is even harder. We tend to assume that the most ambitious people in an organisation will aspire to leadership roles because they crave the opportunity to influence decisions and exercise power. In a law firm, however, taking on a leadership position can potentially entail losing power. In any organisation, as in most areas of life, power comes from controlling access to valuable resources. In a law firm, or indeed in any professional service firm, the most valuable resources are specialist professional expertise and lucrative client relationships. Lawyers who take on major leadership roles necessarily reduce their fee-earning work and may find their hard-won client relationships migrating to their colleagues, or to other firms. By taking time away from frontline client work, they will struggle to ensure that their professional expertise remains at the cutting edge. Of course the idiosyncrasies of each law firm's governance structure will determine the leaders' formal authority and the personal credibility of each individual will determine their informal authority, but the same basic conundrum applies. Individuals who take on leadership roles in law firms risk exchanging their most valuable assets (ie, their client relationships and professional expertise) for a title which brings with it relatively little formal authority but a great deal of responsibility. (Laura Empson, "Leadership, power, and politics in law firms" in Rebecca Normand-Hochman (ed), *Leadership for Lawyers*, International Bar Association, 2015).

In my view, there is an opportunity for a new or old law firm with the courage to model ESG behaviour to build a substantial, sustainable ESG practice. But law firms won't fool GCs with shallow bolt-on ESG offerings to their menu of services without a nuanced approach to ESG in their own firm and to their firm's organisational purpose in the context of society at large.

GCs must become ESG-caring CEOs of their own internal break-even legal services business. They must understand how ESG fits with business strategy and then tell, not ask, the business how they will enable better ESG decisions through excellent legal counsel and process. Then they must not repeat the mistake of many GCs, which is to perform the 'diving catch' on ESG and promise to deliver outcomes which the business has not fully funded.

Finally, the Solicitors Regulation Authority must create an environment in which GCs can stand up to CEOs, CXOs and NEDs whenever the board is baulking at taking good ESG-based decisions because of the negative impact on the bottom line. If there had been money in ESG, everyone would have been doing it long before now. Serious ESG conduct – behaviour over time – will cost money, and GCs can hold directors' feet to the fire on this. But they need support from the regulator, as Professor Stephen Mayson pointed out in his Independent Review of Legal Services Regulation in 2020.

The Centre for Ethics and Law, University College London, published a report on 11 June 2020 written by Professor Stephen Mayson with the title "Reforming legal services – regulation beyond the echo chambers – the final report of the independent review of legal services regulation".

Section 4.12 relates to "Corporate legal departments and in-house lawyers" and in respect of which he makes a recommendation, Recommendation 20, as follows:

> *An in-house legal department should be capable, for regulatory purposes, of being registered as a distinct business unit, so that the*

department's delivery of legal services would be subject to the same regulatory obligations as any other registered provider. Individuals within such a registered in-house unit should also be registered personally if they carry on activities for which before-the-event authorisation or personal accreditation would otherwise be required.

Professor Mayson sets out his reasons for this recommendation as follows:

There is little doubt that a tension is inherent in this relationship when the client for legal services is also the adviser's employer. The usual expectation of 'independent' legal advice is often stretched ... [It is] arguable that those with professional obligations might benefit from further regulatory support ... In principle, they should not be at risk of dismissal or disadvantage simply for observing their professional obligations ... This might entail express conditions in their employment contract, and a direct reporting line to the board ... As we have seen in recent years, corporate failures can lead to consumer and societal detriment. In-house lawyers have to be able to sound alarm bells without the chilling effect of potential reprisal. ...

The words "chilling effect of potential reprisal" are indeed chilling when you consider the impact of corporate failures on society and which failures, more often than not, hit the more vulnerable parts of society.

Sadly, it isn't easy to see how ESG can succeed unless law firms, GCs and the regulator come together to ensure it.

Notes

1   First published in *Modern Lawyer*, published by Globe Law and Business, October 2021. For further information visit: www.globelawandbusiness.com/journals/Modern-Lawyer-Journal.

Appendix 3: Strengthening governance through in-house lawyer independence

First published on Jenifer Swallow's blog, June 2022

(www.jeniferswallow.com/posts/in-house-lawyer-independence-
employment-amendment-letter)

A note for in-house lawyers and their employers

In-house lawyers play a key role in their organisations, bringing much to their work, including beyond their core legal experience. But their primary role is to practise law. They are bound by specific regulatory and professional obligations, which include a duty to act with independence, and to give precedence to their professional obligations over the interests of their client employer.

Recent corporate scandals have put in-house regulation and practice in the spotlight, highlighting the tension between in-house lawyers' requirement of independence and their status as an employee. The Solicitors Regulation Authority, the leading UK legal services regulator, is carrying out a thematic review of the in-house legal role. ESG issues are high on the corporate agenda, holding organisations to adopt ever higher standards of governance and societal responsibility.

To respond to these circumstances and get ahead of the risks, a practical step in-house lawyers and business leaders can take is to acknowledge in writing the regulatory obligations of in-house lawyers via an amendment to their employment contract. This is particularly pertinent for the General Counsel or Chief Legal Officer, but is relevant to all in-house lawyers.

We provide below a template amendment letter, sample talking points and board briefing paper, to make this step easy for in-house lawyers and business leaders to take.

Feedback is welcome at jenifer@jeniferswallow.com and cfenton@ciaranfenton.com.

Jenifer Swallow, a lawyer, and Ciarán Fenton, a leadership and board consultant.

(June 2022)

- - -

Steps
- Request an amendment to the in-house lawyer employment contract to reflect their regulatory duties.
- Use the talking points below in support of this request.
- Prepare and sign the contract amendment letter.
- Send a short briefing paper to the board – see sample below – or discuss at a board development session or meeting.
- Consider also circulating a summary to the wider organisation or covering verbally at a company meeting.

Talking points
- In-house lawyer regulation and practice is in the spotlight. See Discussion Paper.[1]
- The Post Office Scandal is one of a number of examples illustrating what can go wrong for society, business and for lawyers. These issues are set out on The Post Office Horizon IT Inquiry website.

- Corporate responsibility/ESG are high on the public agenda. This is reflected in the investment businesses and law firms are making in ESG practices and content on their websites.
- The Solicitors Regulation Authority, the leading legal services regulator, is carrying out a thematic risk review of in-house solicitors.
- It is straightforward to help organisations to address these risks via a short letter amending the in-house lawyer employment contract. This would outline what is already the case at law, including the in-house lawyer's regulatory responsibilities to act with independence, integrity and in the public interest.
- To further strengthen the position, it is also an option to implement a best practice governance protocol for General Counsel working with boards. This involves:
  - A reporting line for the GC to the senior independent director. This can be in addition to the operational reporting line already in place.
  - A demonstration of the independence of the GC by ensuring that the GC/successor GC's appointment and removal is a decision for the board. This is a similar approach used for Company Secretaries and Data Protection Officers.

TEMPLATE EMPLOYMENT AMENDMENT LETTER
HEADED PAPER
[ADDRESS OF IN-HOUSE COUNSEL]
[DATE]
Dear [NAME]

Acknowledging your regulated status via an amendment to your employment contract

This letter is to confirm that in addition to the terms of your employment contract dated [DATE], we acknowledge that in your employment as a lawyer in our organisation, you are an authorised person, regulated by the Solicitors Regulation Authority, and required in your practice to act:

- in a way that upholds the constitutional principle of the rule of law, and the proper administration of justice
- in a way that upholds public trust and confidence in the solicitors' profession and in legal services provided by authorised persons
- with independence
- with honesty
- with integrity
- in a way that encourages equality, diversity, and inclusion
- in the best interests of each client

[DRAFTING NOTE: replace with applicable regulator and principles if different to the SRA]

We support you meeting these requirements.

This letter shall form part of your employment contract, the other terms of which remain unchanged by this letter.

We each indicate our agreement to the above by signing below.

Yours sincerely

[NAME], [TITLE], on behalf of [LEGAL ENTITY]	Date

[NAME]	Date

[NOTE: consider signing as a deed with witnesses due to no consideration]

SAMPLE BOARD PAPER

Subject	Reducing our risks through in-house lawyer independence
Submitted by	[Name]
Board action required	Discussion and minuting
Date	[Date]

Summary

This paper is in response to a thematic review by a legal services regulator into in-house lawyer independence, and increased focus on governance following recent corporate scandals. We are responding by noting the regulatory obligations our General Counsel is bound by in their work within our organisation. We have acknowledged these obligations via an update to their employment contract, and the contracts of our wider in-house legal team.

Details

The role and purpose of our in-house lawyers is to support effective decision making and operations, to help achieve our organisational purpose and discharge our legal duties.

In fulfilling this role, our lawyers are bound by specific regulatory and professional obligations, including a duty to act with independence. This means their professional obligations ultimately take precedence over our interests as a business. Similar principles apply to other senior staff, eg, our Data Protection Officer and Financial Controller.

Recent corporate scandals have put in-house regulation and practice in the spotlight. The Solicitors Regulation Authority, the leading UK legal services regulator, is carrying out a thematic review of the in-house legal role. ESG issues are high on the corporate agenda, holding organisations to adopt ever higher standards of governance and societal responsibility.

To respond to these circumstances and get ahead of the risks, a practical step we have chosen to take is to acknowledge in writing the regulatory obligations of our in-house lawyers, via an amendment to their employment contract.

We have done this via an amending letter to the employment contracts of our General Counsel and in-house lawyers. These letters acknowledge that as a lawyer in our organisation, they are an 'authorised person', under the remit of the relevant legal services regulator, and required in their practice to act:
- in a way that upholds the constitutional principle of the rule of law, and the proper administration of justice;
- in a way that upholds public trust and confidence in the solicitors' profession and in legal services provided by authorised persons;
- with independence;
- with honesty;
- with integrity;
- in a way that encourages equality, diversity and inclusion; and
- in the best interests of each client.

We confirm in the letter that we support them in meeting these requirements. The letter now forms part of their employment contracts, the other terms of which remain unchanged by the letter. This step helps us achieve our purpose by strengthening our governance, reducing our risks, and helping meet our ESG obligations.

We also highlight to the board that the Legal function needs to have adequate budget and resourcing, access to and profile across the organisation, and presence at the leadership table, to enable it to meet its regulatory obligations and to mitigate the risk of our organisation failing to meet its objectives and/or being exposed to serious conduct and other risk events, including exposure to individual directors.

We also draw your attention to a best practice governance protocol for General Counsel working with boards, which we recommend implementing. This includes:

- A reporting line for the GC to the senior independent director to further support governance.
- A demonstration of the independence of the GC by ensuring their appointment and removal (and that of any successor) is a decision for the board. This is a similar approach used for Company Secretaries and Data Protection Officers.

Action

We will minute the board discussion on these matters and highlight the principles with the wider organisation.

Notes

1   https://docs.google.com/document/d/e/2PACX-1vTJztI9NyoWpW-E2F6yaMYZ6CHBtDKa75pbF2JMruAOtCxo56dj4VhlhQqcA44Gm48DDEaVMEx-twfw/pub.

Appendix 4: GC Response to SRA In-house Solicitors Thematic Review

First published on social media in March 2023

(https://docs.google.com/document/d/e/2PACX-1vTsOgvh0qvOWK_kFXUUnqBct5bxHQuV3jzhDU9QwSbUUY59rJx4vjD1Pc5e9RSbZOt94emhyTrWNERS/pub)

Overview

As leaders in the in-house legal community who have considered deeply the role of in-house lawyers and the positive impact they can have in society, we welcome the recent focus by the Solicitors Regulation Authority on in-house solicitors. We are extremely concerned by the findings of the SRA In-house Solicitors Thematic Review. We are particularly troubled by the fact that the SRA does not appear to see the extent of the challenges for in-house solicitors that the Review signals.

As the Review acknowledges, the in-house legal community has significant influence and value, with 34,500 solicitors contributing to the growth and resilience of 6,000 organisations, and General Counsel serving an important leadership role in corporate decision making and risk mitigation.

The Review understates the severity of the risks present in the in-house environment and misinterprets or is inadequate in its conclusions as to their cause. It does not reflect the collective experience in-house or what was communicated by and to a number of us during the Review, and it offers insufficient action and support in addressing concerns in the interests of stakeholders and society. The data gathered is useful, but the Review's conclusions are not supported by that data.

The purpose of this document is to set out our concerns, along with suggested steps and support we would like the SRA to provide. The aim of our recommendations is to increase regulatory and practical support for General Counsel and in-house lawyers, in order to enable the delivery of better outcomes for society than is currently the case, where the choice is for the lawyer to resign or comply in conflict with their professional and regulatory obligations.

In summary, our request is to (1) acknowledge and prioritise the seriousness of the risks and challenges in the in-house environment, and (2) provide practical, dedicated, well-resourced support to address these risks on an ongoing basis. We offer our support in the taking of these actions.

Key concerns

The Chief Executive of the SRA concludes:
- the Review findings are encouraging
- regulatory risks identified in the in-house community are a minority issue
- risks relate to workloads and lack of training leading to poor decision making

The findings of this review are generally encouraging – most in-house solicitors appear to be able to serve their employers well while still upholding the high standards expected of them. Yet a minority struggle. We heard frequently that heavy workloads were a significant challenge. That is a problem if it means some in-house solicitors struggle to commit appropriate time to training or careful consideration of key decisions. **Paul Philip, SRA Chief Executive**

We cannot agree with these conclusions. It is common for in-house lawyers to face ethical challenges and pressure to compromise their regulatory obligations. This is not a minority issue. To conclude otherwise indicates underreporting, undue optimism and or other deficiencies in the Review.

Underreporting is likely for a range of reasons, including low levels of recognition of the issues by interviewees, potentially narrow or leading framing of survey and interview questions, or presenting a confident view to the regulator upon which your career relies. Optimism is understood to be tempting, with corporate regulatory risks having been largely ignored by the SRA until now, alongside pressure to show things are in hand.

The optimistic tenor of the Review is also inconsistent with statements within it. For example:

> *Many in-house solicitors described experiencing commercial and political pressures and professional isolation. We were also concerned that in most teams there were some weaknesses in policies and controls which would help them to oversee and identify risks. In particular, we noted that balancing regulatory responsibilities and independence while safeguarding effective working relationships could be challenging. These challenges may be exacerbated if in-house teams have limited resources and a lack of focus on ethics in day-to-day learning and work activities.*

These are extremely serious statements to make about a profession upon which so many rely and that has such a critical influence on the success and responsibility of our businesses and institutions.

The Review references twenty-seven risk indicators across five categories of risk, with indicators overlapping such categories. Our initial evaluation based on data available in the Review, is that they most, if not all, indicate significant or moderate likelihood of harm. Given the role of in-house lawyers, that harm has the potential to be material.

The picture painted by the risk indicators is in no way 'encouraging', even with the data points underreported as we see it. The tone and conclusions of the Review suggest the SRA does not view these risk indicators with the same concern and priority as we do.

For example, independence is at the very heart of the tension in the client-employer relationship in-house and yet 64% of in-house solicitors are not raising their regulatory duties including the duty of independence with their client-employers. One in ten experience pressure to compromise their regulatory obligations. 50% of General Counsel feel isolated. Many in-house solicitors are overwhelmed and have inadequate board support. This should be a real cause for concern.

As another example, an in-house solicitor may express they are comfortable saying 'no' when under ethical pressure but to what extent are they able to do so when a particular situation arises, given the array of direct and indirect pressures they may be under? Would any solicitor in such circumstances feel 'comfortable' and is it correct to frame the question in this way? Rather than taking a statistic at face value or as reassurance, we feel an indicator such as this needs further research until it is properly understood across the in-house population, with a mitigation plan to assure the correct governance, infrastructure and support are in place for any solicitor in such circumstances to be able to meet their professional and regulatory obligations in full, without fear or compromise. This is clearly a matter for regulatory concern and action, not solely an issue for an individual solicitor to handle alone.

Regarding the Review data itself on 'saying no' due to ethical concerns, even notwithstanding under-reporting, one in fifty in-house solicitors not speaking out when needed is 680 in-house solicitors across England and Wales. The implications of this are likely to be significant.

Similarly, inadequate resourcing is considered a critical risk in compliance environments such as financial services. To have one in three in-house solicitors struggling to obtain sufficient resource to discharge their duties is a red flag that needs understanding and addressing.

There are also data points that appear to be missing, either where a risk indicator is referenced but no data is provided, or where a risk indicator is implied. For example, it is common in-house to be asked to act in the interests of individual business leaders, rather than in the best interests of the client-employer and it is also common for in-house lawyers to need support in recognising and dealing with this. The same goes for the duty to ensure a client-employer is correctly apprised of all information material to its interests – is this institutionalised in governance or is relevant information not reaching the client because it is not reported above the executive team to the board? It is unclear the level to which these aspects were evaluated in the Review.

It is also well established that financial pressures influence ethics and decision making and most would find it difficult domestically to accommodate a binary or subtle decision between enabling a course of action or resigning. Yet factors relating to financial independence do not appear to have been explored in any detail in the Review.

Suggested action and mitigations

We request the SRA re-evaluate the tone and conclusions of the Review, to ensure the risks are correctly understood, framed and addressed, and with perceived as well as actual priority and urgency. Any gaps in understanding and potential bias in the Review also need to be identified and addressed. We are happy to support in any way to ensure the Review better reflects the reality for GCs and in-house solicitors inside companies and institutions. The same offer stands for other regulators whose regulated community operates in-house, for example the Bar Standards Board.

We see it as critical that the SRA implements a full programme of mitigation, to support in-house solicitors to maintain their professional and regulatory obligations, including their duty of independence, addressing all risk indicators identified and tracking progress over time. In-house solicitors, their clients and stakeholders need this from the regulator.

Including 'next steps to consider' for in-house solicitors in the Review document, with resource links for the client-employer, will be vastly insufficient in response to the risks identified. Regulatory duties need to be clear in practice and have the backing of the regulator. Training and dedicated in-house website resources are a critical part of risk mitigation, alongside awareness raising and events to address the wide-reaching cultural aspects of these issues. It is great to see those planned, but they must be framed in a way that is practical and useful, reach every corner of the in-house legal community and beyond, and do so on an ongoing basis, across all risk areas identified. Specifically we request dedicated published guidance for in-house solicitors on applying the current professional and regulatory framework in their corporate and institutional environments. We offer our support in the preparation and delivery of these materials. However, these actions alone are insufficient.

We further recommend as follows, with immediate term actions indicated with an asterisk.

1. Client-employer engagement

* Active outreach to the CEO and boards of client-employers, as is common in other regulated environments, eg, on appointment of an in-house solicitor (notified via the My SRA website) and at annual practising certificate renewal. This could be done via a template SRA letter outlining regulatory requirements of in-house solicitors, including the duty of independence, and providing access to further resources.

Explore mechanisms for providing regulator backing to in-house solicitors when they need it, eg, letters of support to client-employers or availability for discussion with client-employers about the scope of in-house regulatory duties.

Note: We consider client-employer education, outreach and recognition to be of great importance and there are a range of actions the SRA can take without having regulatory remit over the client-employer entity.

2. Contract terms

* Recommend or require a summary of professional duties is included in employment terms, which can form the basis of or sit alongside solicitor-client terms of engagement referenced in the Review. Professor Stephen Mayson's Independent Review of Legal Services Regulation included recommendations relating to employment terms, amongst other aspects, and Ciarán Fenton and Jenifer Swallow have proposed an employment amendment letter template.

3. Governance

* Introduce SRA recommendations such as regarding board engagement,[1] reporting structure, and recording regulatory and ethics risks.

Engage with the audit profession and recommend to the large accounting firms that they test the efficacy of (1) ethics and reporting, (2) governance structures relating to in-house lawyers, eg, reporting line of the GC, (3) the in-house legal function more broadly, through the audit lens.

Engage with bodies such as the Financial Conduct Authority, Prudential Regulation Authority, Financial Reporting Council, Institute of Chartered Accountants, National Association of Data Protection and Freedom of Information Officers, and the Chartered Governance Institute (formerly the Institute of Chartered Secretaries and Administrators) on the regulatory and professional duties of solicitors, the risk interdependencies and commonalities across regulated professionals working in-house and the measures and support necessary to discharge those duties and mitigate risks. The Regulatory Response Unit could be extended from a technology-focused remit to serve as a wider forum for collaboration and the development, communication and refinement of standards.

4. Wellbeing

Undertake research on (a) the root causes of wellbeing issues that contribute to regulatory risks, including a solicitor's ability to withstand undue/unethical exertions by the client-employer; and (b) the measures that would address those issues, factoring in wider industry research[2] that indicates excessive workloads for in-house solicitors is a significant and growing issue.

Undertake research on the relationship between remuneration, solicitor independence and wellbeing in-house and any best practice structures and thresholds that flow from that research.

5. Annual certification

* Provide reminders and require annual certification regarding professional duties and ethics, eg, as part of annual practising certificate renewal. Note: The changes to renewal requirements have made it easier to skip over the need for ongoing training and removed the ability for in-house lawyers to point to a specific regulatory obligation or process to secure budget and time for training.

6. Community discourse

Encourage community discourse and support across key risk areas, including in regards the role, responsibility and support of external counsel.

Coordinate with the Law Society and other relevant bodies to ensure cohesive communications and activity.

7. Enforcement

Publish focused in-house investigation and enforcement activity to assure focus, illustrate red lines and instil confidence in standards.

Additionally, to mitigate the Review being ineffectual or counterproductive in addressing regulatory risks and SRA objectives, we recommend as follows:

Ensure well-resourced follow up activity that reaches all relevant parties so this is not seen as a 'one and done' or token exercise or something that reaches only a minority.

Commission an independent expert (such as Professor Richard Moorhead) to undertake a detailed evaluation of data and risks identified in the Review.

Provide the following information to enable further public evaluation:
- The survey and interview questions.
- The anonymised data analytics from the survey and interviews, including range and representation of respondents.
- Any bias evaluation that was undertaken in relation to sampling and assessment.
- Any research or statistics outside the survey and interviews that contributed to the findings in the Review.
- The SRA's risk evaluation and mitigation plan following the Review.

Conclusion

The Review represents a significant opportunity to give the in-house legal working environment the attention it needs and deserves, and for which many in-house solicitors are desperate. There is much that is fantastic about the in-house legal world, but there are also systemic issues – as is the case in any sector. Identifying, acknowledging and tackling these head on has the potential to strengthen resilience and effective decision making within our corporations and institutions, help reduce corporate misconduct, and stimulate growth and a fresh approach into the future. With high profile cases such as the Post Office Horizon Scandal under review, and other corporate failings in the public domain including RICS, P&O Ferries, Rolls Royce, deferred prosecutions at banks, misuse of NDAs and more, downplaying concerns delays this opportunity at a time when public trust in lawyers is both needed and in question. It also undermines confidence within the in-house legal community in their regulator and robs them of the support they need.

The aim of our recommendations is to increase regulatory support for General Counsel and in-house lawyers in the service of society, without the only choice being to resign or conform in conflict with professional and regulatory obligations.

We welcome the focus of the SRA on the in-house community and encourage this focus to be maximised, not wasted, even (and especially) if that means facing into discomfort.

We are at the disposal of the SRA to discuss any and all aspects of this document or the Review, and to support in any way we can in strengthening the environment around in-house solicitors, to enable them to meet their professional and regulatory duties to their client-employers and wider society, and to not have to compromise their wellbeing along the way.

Shanika Amarasekara	Angélique Parisot-Potter
Nilema Bhakta-Jones	Stacey Quaye
Vanessa Cowling	James Richardson
Maaike de Bie	Polly Russell Stower
Russell Deards	Allison Sandle
Elizabeth Dyce	Benjamin White
Paul Gilbert	Nick Hartigan
Richard Given	Manu Kanwar
Lucie Grant	Bruce Macmillan
Jamie Fraser	Andrew Mills
Hazel Butler	Elizabeth O'Niell
Jill Byron	Solomon Osagie
Andrew Cooke	James Sullivan
Pav Gill	Jenifer Swallow
Adam Hirschovits	Lesley Wan
Peter Ho	Ben Watts
Ian Illersic	

Notes

1   Eg, Moorhead, Richard Lewis and Clark, Trevor and Brener, Alan and Gilbert, Paul and Vaughan, Steven, *In-House Lawyers and Non-Executive Directors: A Discussion About Best Practice* (27 June 2019), https://papers.ssrn.com/sol3/papers.cfm?abstract_id=3410929.
2   Eg, www.axiomlaw.com/2023-uk-deputy-general-counsel-report, www.ibanet.org/Mental-wellbeing-in-the-legal-profession, www.lawcare.org.uk/life-in-the-law/.

About the author

Ciarán Fenton
Leadership consultant and board facilitator
cfenton@ciaranfenton.com

Ciarán Fenton is a leadership consultant, board facilitator and writer/speaker on managing relationships at work, ESG and creating sustainable organisations. He facilitates improved decision making within boards by exploring the interdependence between the personal purpose, strategy and behaviour (PSB) plan of each board member and that of their organisation.

Since 2002 he has worked with individuals and organisations using an approach to self-management that he has developed over many years based on his personal and organisational experiences. It provides senior leaders with the thinking and tools to achieve a small change in their behaviour, and that of each member of their team, by negotiating productive relationship contracts with each other.

During his early career he held senior business leadership roles at Hachette, ITN, Pearson and The Guardian Media Group in which he was involved in change programmes. Ciarán is a mentor at London Business School's Entrepreneurship Summer School, a faculty member on Paul Gilbert's LBCambridge2 senior in-house counsel programme, and a speaker on creating sustainable organisations including at the Cambridge Institute for Sustainability Leadership (CISL).

In 2022 he was diagnosed with lymphoma and had extensive chemotherapy and a stem cell transplant leading to remission. He feels that experience changed him, his purpose and his approach to his work, speaking and writing. He holds a business degree from the National University of Ireland, Cork. He is married to the writer Marian Garvey and they have two children.

About Globe Law and Business

Globe Law and Business was established in 2005. From the very beginning, we set out to create legal books that are sufficiently high level to be of real use to the experienced professional, yet still accessible and easy to navigate. Most of our authors are drawn from Magic Circle and other top commercial firms, both in the United Kingdom and internationally.

Our titles are carefully produced, with the utmost attention paid to editorial, design and production processes. We hope this results in high-quality publications that are easy to read and a pleasure to own.

In 2021, we were very pleased to announce the start of a new chapter for Globe Law and Business following the acquisition of law books under the imprint Ark Publishing. Our law firm management list is now significantly expanded with many well-known and loved Ark Publishing titles.

We are also pleased to announce the launch of our online content platform, Globe Law Online. This allows for easy search and networked access across firms. Key collections include the Law Firm Management Collection. Details of all titles included can be found at www.globelawonline.com. Email glo@globelawandbusiness.com for further details and to arrange a free trial for you or your firm.

We'd very much like to hear from you with your thoughts and ideas for improving what we offer. Please do feel free to email me at sian@globelawandbusiness.com. Happy reading and thank you for your time.

Sian O'Neill
Managing director
Globe Law and Business
www.globelawandbusiness.com